PLANNING & M

SMALL
GARDEN

PLANNING & MAKING A
SMALL GARDEN

Alan Toogood

WARD LOCK LIMITED · LONDON

ACKNOWLEDGEMENTS

The publishers gratefully acknowledge the following agencies for granting permission to reproduce the following colour photographs: Pat Brindley (pp. 39 (lower), 71 (lower)); Harry Smith Horticultural Photographic Collection (pp. 2, 31 (lower), 43 (upper), 51 (upper), 59, 71 (upper) and 78). The photographs on the cover and on pp. 9, 31 (upper), 43 (lower), 51 (lower) and 90 were taken by Bob Challinor; that on p. 63 was taken by Frank Hermann.

All the line drawings are by Nils Solberg.

Front cover: courtesy Harry Smith Horticultural Photographic Collection.

First published in Great Britain in 1987
by Ward Lock Limited, 8 Clifford Street
London W1X 1RB, an Egmont Company

House editor Denis Ingram

Text filmset in Bembo
by Hourds Typographica, Stafford

Printed and bound in Portugal
by Resopal

British Library Cataloguing in Publication Data

Toogood, Alan R.
  Planning and making a small garden.
    1. Gardens
    I. Title
    712'.6   SB453

ISBN 0-7063-6625-5

Frontispiece: Several distinctive features can be included in small gardens. For instance, pools are very popular today and easily constructed, as are pergolas for climbing plants. An irregular-shaped lawn helps to make a square or rectangular plot more interesting.

CONTENTS

PREFACE

Designing and creating a garden should be fun and you certainly do not need to be a professional designer to have a well laid out garden. All you need are plenty of ideas and some sample plans to get you started. The newcomer to gardening, whether faced with a brand new plot as left by the builders, or with an established but perhaps neglected garden, will find plenty of inspiration in these pages.

You are guided gently through clearing the site and how to plan it on paper; advice on choosing all the features that you are likely to require (from patios, pergolas, lawns and screens, to planting schemes such as heather and conifer beds and ground cover) follows.

The garden plans and colour photographs will give you many ideas for laying out your garden, whether you want a simple, labour-saving plot or a more complex garden where you can really indulge in gardening. Gardens for town and country are considered, and difficult sites are also covered.

Hints are given on constructing many of the garden features described, sufficient to enable you to tackle the practicalities of creating a garden, but in-depth guidance has been played down, for basically this is an ideas book, written to stimulate the imagination!

A.T.

CHAPTER I

THE MODERN GARDEN

There has never been such an exciting time for gardeners. The modern garden is the outcome of centuries of evolution and development. All that is best from the past has been kept, all that is least acceptable to modern ideas discarded. Gardens are not as large as they were in the past but the potential for making them more beautiful and easier to maintain has vastly improved.

Gardens have been enriched not only by the treasures brought back by intrepid plant-collectors of the nineteenth and twentieth centuries from America, China, Japan, the Himalayas, Australia, New Zealand and other parts of the world, but also by the highly skilled labours of hybridizers or plant breeders. There has never been such a wealth of plants from which to create colourful and fruitful gardens. The same is true of garden design, where not only can one draw on the best ideas of the great traditions of Europe and America, but also on those of such countries as Japan.

All gardeners must be influenced by the past which lives on in the gardens of great country houses and to a large extent in public parks, and do their best to marry the traditional with the taste and requirements of today. To this end there are aids available of which our forebears never dreamed. And those who supply us with plants and seeds will tell us that we have an ever-increasing appetite for novelty and improvement in all kinds of garden plants!

The gardener, too, has changed with the times. If we were to seek today's typical gardener we would find him or her looking after a suburban 'front and back' in which up to two-thirds of the area is devoted to lawn, and the rest mainly to flowers, roses, flowering shrubs and possibly some vegetables and fruit. Our gardener will be equipped with an armoury of aids, some traditional, others very modern.

ELEMENTS OF THE MODERN GARDEN

So let us look more closely at the components of a pleasing and useful garden. There is no set formula, but some features are common to most gardens. A garden without flowers is unthinkable, at least for the area that can be seen from the house. And until recently the design was not complete without a lawn – often two. Today, however, paving and other hard surfaces are no longer restricted to paths and service areas.

Imaginative use is being made of pre-formed concrete slabs, cobbles, granite setts, gravel, timber decking and bricks as labour-saving ground-work, relieved by formal beds and perhaps a fish pool or statue. Such modern garden design is particularly appropriate in the context of the 'town house' terrace. This architectural approach has brought with it a new interest in the form and texture of plants, which accounts for the growing sales by nurseries and garden centres of dwarf evergreens and compact shrubs with grey, silver and variegated foliage.

However, for the majority a green lawn remains the perfect restful foil, with improved machines to take the toil out of mowing – and there are even powered edging machines to give that clean finish without any effort. The balance of herbaceous border flowers, bedding plants and bulbs depends so much on personal preference – though most of us will pack in as many of each as space, time and ready cash allow. Selection and management of these plants is covered in later sections. Flowers need no general words of commendation, but it can be said that flowering and foliage shrubs still remain relatively neglected, while ornamental trees come lower still on the garden-maker's list of priorities.

It is true that for a couple of weeks in spring gardens are gay with golden-yellow forsythia, pink cherry, berberis and the very modest pink or red of ribes – followed very much later by an autumn blaze of berries from cotoneaster and pyrancantha. But this is just a scratch at the surface. The rose is regarded as a shrub and is justly a firm favourite. Yet it is so easy to be wooed by those who wish to sell only large-flowered (hybrid tea) and cluster-flowered (floribunda) roses, to the exclusion of the informal beauty of the shrub roses and the delightful older climbers and ramblers that clothe walls, fences, arches and doorways so well. In recent years, with gardens becoming smaller, there has been a surge of interest in miniature roses, ideally suited to small beds, for edging borders and for planting in ornamental containers.

Generally speaking shrubs will look after themselves if kept in proportion by restrained use of secateurs. Fruit trees are ornamental as well as productive. Newcomers to gardening tend to avoid them, but those grown for garden planting today are nearly all raised on rootstocks that impart a dwarf habit and slow growth so there is little fear that they will get out of hand. Bush fruit is easy to manage and the new gardener is well advised to plant some of the types that rarely appear in fruit shops today – such as red and white currants. They will not take up much space if specially trained, while a row of raspberries can make a useful and quite attractive screen between 'kitchen' and 'pleasure' areas.

Vegetable gardening has cast off its gloomy, cloth-cap war-time image and is become an interesting and rewarding pastime. So consider allocating an area to a rotation of 'salads', 'roots' and 'greens'. Many gardeners today need no persuasion to grow herbs, which are charming in growth and piquant in the pot: it's best to allocate them a special bed near the kitchen or even to maintain them on the windowsill in pots or a box.

SOIL, SITE AND CLIMATE

Any gardener must be a realist and respect the limitations of the site while, at the same time, using all his or her resources to overcome problems. For example, on a windswept hillside there will be constant damage to all but the lowest growing plants until a screen is provided to filter the prevailing wind. This may be in the form of a trelliswork screen, hedge or group of trees – and must be considered a priority. Disappointment will be inevitable if the gardener insists on trying to grow the more tender shrubs in exposed northern districts, just as extremes of dryness in a sunny situation or shade cast by buildings or trees will limit the growth of a wider range of plants.

Other considerations are the size, shape and slope of the site. A little, but not much, can be done to counter the influence of local topography and climate on the garden, but the native soil is another matter altogether. Its type will certainly influence the character of the garden, but you should not admit defeat because you have, for example, inhospitable clay, sand or chalk. The degree of acidity or alkalinity will influence what can be grown – in a lime-rich soil the rhododendron tribe will never be happy and hydrangeas will be pink rather than blue. Slight acidity suits the majority of garden plants, while the inclusion of peat, organic matter from compost heaps, animal manure and acidic fertilizers will all ameliorate excess alkalinity.

PLANNING ON PAPER

The pleasant task of garden-making always begins on paper – graph paper – on which a scale plan is drawn. The larger the paper, the easier and more accurate the draughtsmanship. Start by measuring the outside perimeter of the house and then choose a scale that will enable the whole site area to fit on paper: 1.2 or 1.8 m to 2.5 cm (4 or 8 ft to 1 in) is often

Above In this rectangular garden a curved lawn helps to create the impression of greater width. The dense planting of shrubs helps to conceal the boundary and makes for a labour-saving yet colourful border.

Right Most people will want to grow roses, but in a small garden they are best grouped with perennials, especially grey-foliage kinds, and with other shrubs, as rose beds are very dull in winter.

used. Some rudimentary surveying equipment is required, the basics being a stout tape measure, a couple of long lines of cord, nylon or wire, half a dozen stout pointed stakes about 30 cm (12 in) long, an equal number of 1.2 m (4 ft) bamboo canes, and a large right-angle triangle made of wood. Take as a base line a wall of the house that faces the greatest part of the garden and run lines at right angles from this wall until they meet the boundary of the site. If the line of sight is impeded, set up canes along the line so that each is exactly in front of the previous one when viewed with the eye close to it. Transfer these maximum distances to the graph paper, marking the boundary points with dots.

From points along these initial lines (marked by canes) run 'branches' at right angles until these lines reach other garden boundaries. Measure the distances and transfer them to the plan. If the garden is on several sides of the house, these house walls must be used as new base lines to make further right-angle measurements. When sufficient dots have been made on the paper they can be joined up to make an accurate perimeter plan of the site. Also measure and mark the position of any tree or other permanent feature that is to be retained.

Draughtsman's tracing paper now comes in useful. Pin a sheet over the graph paper and sketch in possible positions for certain major features – paths, borders, lawn, 'kitchen' area, pool, greenhouse and so on. Over this can be placed another sheet of tracing paper on which variations and other details can be marked in a different colour. In this way a picture of the future garden can be built up and changed until the ideal is achieved. Aim for simplicity and seek a balance between straight lines (as for paths) and sweeping curves (for lawn and border edges). Bear in mind that an 'artistic' design of little beds in grass or winding paths may look nice on paper but that to translate it into spade-work and concrete mixing can be a herculean task at the outset and require constant edging and mainten-ance. Instead, allow for a larger lawn area than you might think you want, and include a large sweeping border instead of scattered beds. Later it will be much easier to cut into the grass area to make another feature (or put additional shrubs in a big border) than to erase items from an over-fussy or time-consuming layout.

While still at the planning stage, some design principles should be noted. To create an effect of greater distance make a focal point, with a tree, sundial or seat for example, at the end of a long view or vista, and let a path 'disappear' behind an internal hedge or trellis. Conversely, to shorten a long site divide the garden into self-contained areas. For example, a circular lawn near the house with a low hollow wall on its far side will concentrate interest on its pleasing proportions so that the eye is less distracted by the length of garden beyond. Most gardens are rectangular, so break the rectangle by curving the edges of lawn and borders.

Above all be realistic: design for easy management. Have good access paths for the mower and other heavy tools; this may mean a slope instead of steps. Consider bringing the food-growing area and greenhouse near the house if ease of access is more important than eye-appeal. Remember that you may want to supply electricity to the greenhouse, or even have a heated frame, and that it is pointless to place a shed at the bottom of the plot and tramp the whole distance for every item that is kept there.

GROUND-WORK

If the garden is on level land there should be no need to move soil in any quantity unless it is to relieve uniform flatness by creating undulations. Ground must often be raised for a rock garden and it can be an economy to plan this in combination with a pool: the excavation for one making the elevation for the other.

On a site where the main garden falls away from the house, a primary task could be to make a terrace against the house for which purpose the ground requires building up. The fall of a site can be broken at any point by building a low wall of stone or brick, moving some soil to the higher level at the same time, and interrupting the wall with a couple of steps. Gardens which slope towards the house clearly present drainage problems. But if the nature of the site demands such an arrangement, strong retaining walls will be needed with seep-holes through which surplus water can flow to rubble drains.

For the lawn a level site is generally preferable though a slight slope will assist drainage. Some soil movement is generally necessary and a cardinal rule is to preserve the valuable top-soil which may get turned during excavation. So shovel away as much top-soil as is practicable from the area of soil movement and keep it heaped near by.

CHAPTER 2

TECHNIQUES OF GARDENING

SURVEYING THE SITE

The first thing to do with any garden is to survey it. This is simple: all you need do initially is walk round your garden and determine what you want to do with it and what the problems are going to be. You will need to take reasonably accurate measurements of the dimensions of the garden so that you can draw precise plans.

In the garden of a newly built house this is usually straightforward. However, if you have bought an old house with an established garden the problems may be rather different. Established gardens are basically of two types: those that have been well maintained and those that have been neglected. If you take on an established garden that has been well maintained the best thing to do is carry on with the maintenance for the first year. This will enable you to find out what is already in the garden, before deciding to make any changes. If, however, you have taken on a neglected garden you may have a lot of clearing to do before you can survey the site: indeed you may have quite a lot to do before you can even establish the boundaries.

SITE CLEARANCE

Clearing the site is an essential operation in all gardens, old and new, but the problems of each are different.

With old overgrown gardens the first thing to do is clear away the dense growth of weeds, brambles, and so on; only when this has been done can you establish the boundaries and the lie of the land. The weeds must be killed off before any cultivations are undertaken. They can be sprayed with a weedkiller containing glyphosate when they are in full growth, following the manufacturer's instructions. When they are dead they should be cut down to ground level. This can be done with a heavy-duty, nylon-line trimmer (the type with interchangeable cutting heads and a petrol-driven motor), or for large areas with a mechanical scythe. You should be able to hire either of these.

Alternatively, you can cut down the dense growth first and then spray the re-growth with glyphosate weedkiller; again when the weeds are in full growth.

An alternative to glyphosate is to use a proprietary brushwood killer, especially recommended if you have a really dense growth of brambles. Bear in mind that when using this you have to allow a specified period to elapse before you can start planting – so follow carefully the maker's instructions.

Any scrubby or tough woody growth, such as old shrubs, should be cut down with long-handled, heavy-duty pruners, or with a pruning saw.

Where small trees need to be removed, first the branches should be sawn off and then most of the trunk, leaving a stump about 1 m (3 ft) high. Next, remove the soil from around the stump to expose the roots, cut through them with a pruning saw and lift out the stump. On no account tackle a large tree, for felling is a highly skilled operation and should be done by professional, qualified arboriculturists or tree surgeons. (The roots of shrubs which have been cut down should be removed in a similar way.)

Once the ground has been cleared it can be dug, if only a small area, ideally using the technique known as double digging (p.23). While digging, remove roots of the dead weeds, brambles, etc. If you have a garden which is too large to dig by hand, hire a heavy-duty rotary culti-vator. After using the machine, go over the ground with a rake or fork removing roots that have been loosened.

The problems that face those who have taken on a garden surrounding a newly built house are rather different. In the first place it is possible that the builder will have removed all your top-soil and left you with only the relatively infertile and intractable sub-soil; in which case you will have to buy in some top-soil from a local supplier. You will need a depth of between 15 and 30 cm (6 and 12 in) over the sub-soil – go for the greater depth if finances allow.

However, do not purchase top-soil until all levelling and changes of level have been made. Where patios, paths and drives are to be made no top-soil will be needed.

Even if the builder has had the kindness to leave your garden with its original top-soil, the chances are that he will also have left you with quite a number of other things, too, such as broken bricks and large slabs of concrete. You may also find that he has buried pieces of corrugated iron, timber, roofing felt, sheets of plastic and other materials incompatible with soil fertility and good drainage. These should be removed.

Where large slabs of concrete occur – as they often do where the site concrete-mixer has been standing – these must be broken up with a sledge hammer, or levered out of the ground with a crow-bar or pick-axe. Concrete and other rubble is worth retaining if you are contemplating laying a drive, paths or patio: it will save having to buy in hardcore.

SOIL

To the non-gardener earth is just earth. It is when you want to start growing things that it begins to take on a rather different character.

Soil is made up of two basic types of material – mineral and organic. The mineral part is the result of vast geological forces that have, with the assistance of weathering over an immense period of time, broken down basic rocks into finer and finer particles. Basically, therefore, the type of soil in any garden will depend very largely on the type of rock in the area. The organic part of soil is what we call humus. This is decayed vegetable and animal matter in the soil. It forms a kind of sponge which retains water and enables plants to acquire essential nutrients from the soil.

There is a third component of soils that is often forgotten: the soil population. This is made up of a surprisingly large number of creatures, some of them beneficial, others regarded as pests. These include not only the obvious creatures such as earthworms, but also a very large number of micro-organisms. The extent of the soil population will depend largely on the amount of humus in the soil: it is the function of the micro-organisms to break down dead creatures and vegetation and release the plant nutrients locked up in them, so that the plants can use them. Thus the overall fertility of any soil depends on the ratios in which these various constituents are combined.

Gardeners recognize a number of different types of soil; each has its own particular advantages and disadvantages.

BASIC SOIL TYPES

Loam This is the ideal soil in relation to structure. It feels smooth without being gritty. It is neither sticky when a moist sample is rubbed in the hand; nor is it powdery. A light loam has more sand in it – over two-thirds. A heavy loam has more clay – over one-third. A medium loam has just the right texture and retains water and food well. It warms up quickly in spring, enabling plants to get away to a good start. If it is very acid it will need dressings of lime (unless you want to grow lime-hating plants). Humus-making manures and garden compost will be needed, as well as fertilizers, even though loams are naturally quite fertile. Lighter dressings than those used for poor soils are generally sufficient for loams.

Sand This is a non-sticky soil even when wet, and people with heavy soils often envy gardeners with sandy types because the latter are so easy to cultivate. But sands are hungry soils, needing a lot of manure, peat, garden compost, and fertilizers. They can become very dry in summer, but warm up quickly in spring, making them ideal for early sowings. Often they are very acid.

Clay A heavy cold soil which is sticky to the touch when wet and binds into unbreakable lumps in dry weather. Drainage generally needs to be improved. Although clay contains a good supply of plant foods, these will need supplementing with fertilizers. Clay soils can be acid and require more liberal liming than loams.

Chalk These soils are rich in lime or chalk and so one cannot grow lime-hating plants such as many heathers, rhododendrons and camellias. The top-soil may be dark and it is generally thin. The sub-soil may be almost pure chalk. Often the ground seems very wet and sticky after it has rained, rather like clay, but then it dries out rapidly, becoming hard and rough to the touch. It is more easily dug in this state. It is important to improve chalky soils with organic, humus-forming matter, like strawy manure, compost, peat, and so on, to help it retain moisture. Mulching will also prevent rapid drying-out in warm weather.

Peat A dark, spongy soil often very rich in plant foods. If it is the fen peat type it will need to have its drainage improved and liming will be necessary as invariably it is far too acid. Peat soils should not be over-limed, however, as this upsets the chemical balance of the soil.

Stony The proverbial infertility of stony ground is due to the fact that moisture drains away rapidly. A few stones in the soil, however, may actually help to retain moisture. It is an almost impossible task to remove all the stones as more seem to surface to take the place of those removed. A better approach is to add plenty of moisture-retaining and rich humus-makers, such as garden compost or manure, together with fertilizers.

SOIL TESTING
To discover the main constituents of a soil all that is required is an empty milk bottle. Dig a narrow hole with a trowel and then remove a slice of

soil from the side to a depth of 7.5–10 cm (3–4 in). Crumble this into the milk bottle. Pour in water to cover the soil and shake the contents well. When this is left to settle, the heavier constituents will fall to the bottom first and the lighter parts will form narrow bands above. This will give an indication of the proportions of grit, sand, silt, clay and organic matter present. Generally speaking, the coarser the particle size, the easier the management of the soil.

Chemical soil analysis is carried out with a soil-test kit which can be purchased from any garden centre. First-stage testing is for acidity or alkalinity. This is generally done by shaking a sample of soil in a special chemical. The colour which the chemical adopts is then compared against a chart showing the degree of acidity or alkalinity. The soil may be neutral – neither acid nor alkaline.

The degree of acidity or alkalinity is measured on what is known as the pH scale, from 0 to 14. The neutral point is 7 on this scale. Soils with a pH of 6.5 and below are acid; those with a pH of 7.5 and above are alkaline (contain chalk or lime). A neutral or slightly acid reaction is a happy state of affairs for general-purpose gardening. Some plants, such as ericas, hydrangeas and rhododendrons thrive on acid soils; others like brassicas (cabbage, etc.) and lilac prefer alkaline soils.

An acid soil is easily made alkaline by adding lime. It is not so easy to make a highly alkaline soil less so; all that one can do is add plenty of peat or garden compost and use acid fertilizers such as sulphate of ammonia.

More sophisticated soil-test kits enable an analysis to be made of plant foods like nitrogen, phosphorus and potash.

DRAINAGE

Most plants need soil that retains moisture yet is able to quickly rid itself of excess water. Very few plants can live with their roots perpetually submerged in stagnant water. Any soil that is waterlogged has little or no air and plants must have air around the roots in order to live.

With soils in which waterlogging or very wet conditions occur, steps must be taken to improve drainage. Usually deep digging (double digging) will improve drainage considerably but sometimes it is necessary to take more drastic steps and install a drainage system (Fig. 1). If a drainage system is required you might find it best to install it during any site levelling that is necessary (p.20).

Today, installing a drainage system need not be hard work. Narrow,

A small garden in which a sense of distance has been created in spite of the fence blocking the view at the far end of the garden.

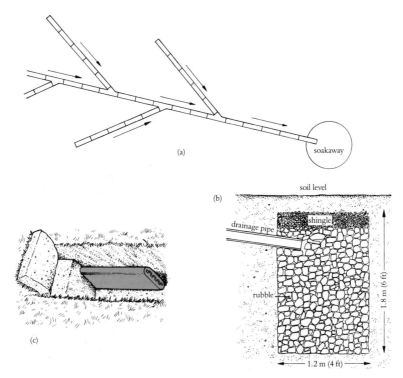

Fig. 1 Drainage systems. Pipes are laid in a herring-bone formation (a), the main pipe leading to a soakaway (b). Some modern land-drainage pipes are very narrow and can be laid in slit trenches (c).

plastic, land-drainage pipes which are simply laid in narrow, slit-like trenches are very easy and quick to use.

To conduct drainage water there must be a gradient. If the garden slopes then take advantage of this to run the drainage pipes to a soakaway at the lowest point. On a level site the drainage pipes must be made to slope – the main drain slopes to the soakaway and lateral drains slope to the main one.

An alternative to plastic land-drainage pipes is to dig trenches about 60 cm (2 ft) deep and to pack them with a 22 cm (9 in) depth of graded rubble.

A single drain across the site is rarely sufficient: a herring-bone pattern of branches, say 4.5 m (15 ft) apart, falling to meet the main drain, should ensure adequate drainage on the most difficult land.

Drainage water is discharged into a rubble-filled soakaway which is dug as deeply as possible at the lowest point. Depth should be at least 1.8 m (6 ft) and preferably more, with a width of at least 1.2 m (4 ft).

SITE LEVELLING

Site levelling is probably the most major task that will ever be undertaken in any garden. It must, therefore, be one of the first operations. If you have a sloping site you may well need one or two level areas — perhaps for a lawn and/or patio. On the other hand, if you have a perfectly level site you may want to introduce a variation in level to relieve the monotony.

The first operation is to remove all the top-soil from the area to be altered. The top-soil is the layer of fertile soil over the lower or sub-soil.

The procedure which follows is the standard method of creating a level area (Fig. 2). Move the sub-soil around as necessary until the site is roughly level to the eye. Then make final adjustments with the aid of wooden pegs, a mallet, a straight-edged board about 1.8 m (6 ft) in length and a spirit-level. At a central spot in the area knock in a peg until the top is level with the ground. Knock in another peg 1.8 m (6 ft) from this and place the board on top of the two. Set the spirit level on the board to check the level. Adjust the second peg until the spirit level shows that it is perfectly level with the first peg. The second peg may either be proud of the ground or slightly below it, so soil must be added or removed accordingly. Proceed in this way all over the site, inserting pegs and moving the soil as necessary with a rake. Finally replace the top-soil.

A slope can be levelled in three ways: by adopting the lowest level and removing all soil above this; by adopting the highest level and importing soil; or by choosing the intermediate level and removing high ground to fill low ground. Unless dramatic changes in level are required, the third alternative is the one requiring least effort and soil upset.

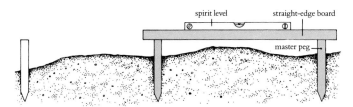

Fig. 2 Land can be levelled by inserting a series of pegs over the site, ensuring the tops are level by means of a straight-edged board and spirit level.

To make a regular slope rather than a flat area, you can again insert a master peg, but at the lowest point. Then use the board and spirit level technique when inserting further pegs, to achieve a regular gradient. The subsequent pegs will be above the level of the master peg.

BORDERS AND BEDS

Having levelled the site or created new levels the next step is to mark out borders and beds, working from your plan (Fig. 3). For square or

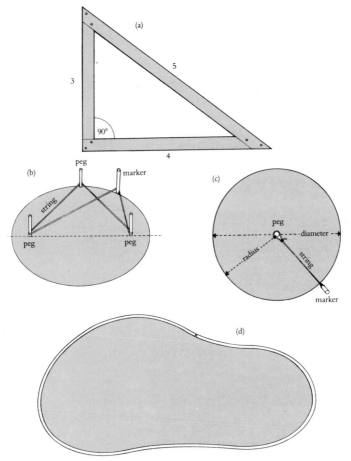

Fig. 3 Marking out beds. (a) A right-angled triangle for marking out perfect corners. (b) A method of marking out an elliptical bed. (c) Circular beds are easily marked out. (d) Irregular shapes can first be formed with a length of hosepipe.

rectangular beds and borders it is useful to have a right-angled frame for getting the corners square. This is easily made by taking three pieces of straight-edged wood and joining them together so that they form a triangle, one corner of which is a right angle.

Curves and circles can be marked out by using a fixed stake with string attached to it, at the other end of which is a pointed stick used for marking. The whole device is used in the same way as a pair of compasses.

To mark out an elliptical bed first decide on the length and width. Using a stake and string (as described above), and using a radius of half the length of the bed, make two curves or arcs on each side of the bed, working from each end of the bed. Where these two curves intersect insert a stake. Then take a length of string of exactly the same length as that of the bed and make a loop in each end. Place the loops over the two stakes at each side of the bed and with a pointed stick held tightly against the string score the outline of the bed in the ground. This should mark out a perfect ellipse of the prescribed length and breadth.

Irregular-shaped beds are easy to mark out – use a length of hosepipe or rope and lay it on the ground to the shape desired. You can achieve beautiful, flowing curves in this way.

Having levelled the site and marked out beds and borders, the next operations are digging and then laying the lawn. Lawns are discussed in Chapter 8.

DIGGING

The purpose of digging is to break up soil to admit air and to allow free drainage of excess water through the soil. Soil that is well aerated and which drains freely is a healthy soil, with a thriving population.

If taken steadily, digging can be one of the most rewarding of all gardening tasks. The type of digging undertaken will depend on the state of the soil. At this stage you will be most concerned about the problems of drainage and the soil structure and type, as discussed earlier.

SINGLE DIGGING
If the top-soil is thin, or the area has already been dug to the depth of two spits (two lengths of the spade blade) it may only be necessary to carry out single digging. This means digging a trench one spit deep and turning over the next strip of soil into it, and so on. The soil from the first trench is taken to the end of the plot being dug and used to fill the final trench. Manure or garden compost should be added to each trench – about a quarter of a barrowload for every 1.2 m (4 ft) length of trench.

It is generally agreed that rough digging of this kind (leaving the ground rough on the surface), is best done in the autumn or winter so that frost penetrates the ground and breaks it up. The soil will then be easy to work in the spring. Digging at this time of year is particularly beneficial to clay soils.

DOUBLE DIGGING

Double digging enables you to improve the drainage of your soil because it extends to two spits, or over 45 cm (18 in). You will be breaking up the sub-soil. This sub-soil is never lifted, but manure or garden compost, and fertilizers, can be forked into it (Fig. 4a).

You take out a wider trench than for single digging – make it 60 cm (2 ft) wide and a spit deep. Take out this trench at one end of the plot and barrow the soil to the other end. Or, you can divide a large plot into two strips and work down to the bottom of one and back up the other. The heap of soil taken from the first trench is placed near to where the last trench will be.

When you have forked over the bottom of the first trench to a spit deep, and added compost or manure, dig a second trench behind the first, turning over the soil into the first one, so that grass and weeds are placed upside down. Alternatively, you can slice off the top like a turf and lay it upside down in the trench and then turn over the rest of the soil on top of

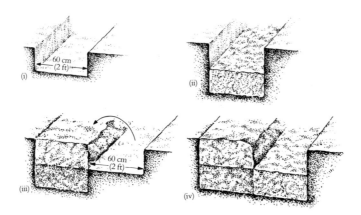

Fig. 4a Double digging. (i) First a wide trench is removed. (ii) Then the bottom is dug over. (iii) A second trench is taken out, throwing the soil forward into the first one. (iv) Again the bottom is dug.

it. Remember to remove roots of perennial weeds, like bindweed, dandelion, ground elder, nettles, couch grass and buttercup, while digging, for if left they will grow again.

Double digging is recommended for all new ground and traditionally is carried out on vegetable plots every three years.

If you decide to use a rotary cultivator instead of hand digging you should set the blades to cultivate to their maximum depth, then go over the whole area. Next spread the manure, compost, etc., and go over the area with the cultivator again, in the transverse direction, to work in the organic matter.

RIDGING

Ridging is a form of digging which exposes a much larger surface area of soil to the frosts, as the ground is thrown up into a series of ridges (Fig. 4b). It is very useful for heavy clays. As before, a trench one spit deep is dug and the soil removed to the other end of the plot. The trench should be about 60 cm (2 ft) wide. When taking out the second trench, three

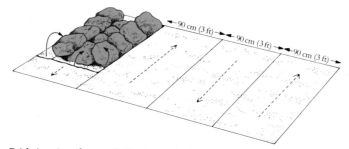

Fig. 4b Ridging is a form of digging which exposes a large surface area of soil to the frosts, as the ground is thrown up into a series of ridges.

spadesful of soil, one behind the other, are turned over into the first trench. The first will be furthest away, the second next to it and the third on top to make a ridge. Alternatively, you can lay the first spadeful in the centre of the trench and the other two at an angle to each other over it, also making a ridge. The plot is made up into lines of ridges in this way.

FERTILIZERS

Just as human beings need different foods, so do plants. There are three major plant foods: nitrogen, phosphorus and potash (N, P and K). Nitrogen encourages green growth, phosphorus helps in root development and potash plays a part in flower and fruit formation.

In addition to these, there are several minor but essential elements needed by plants such as calcium, iron, magnesium, manganese and boron. These occur in sufficient quantities in most properly managed soils. But generally, you need to supply regularly the three major elements.

Under natural conditions there is a cycle by which plants and animals contribute their debris to the soil. This debris is rich in plant foods as well as being bulky, organic material that improves the structure and health of the soil during its decay into humus.

When we cultivate a garden we inevitably interrupt this natural cycle and make great demands on the food reserve of the soil. We tend, for example, to keep ground bare around clumps of flowers and shrubs so that little vegetation returns to the soil. We try to grow several crops of salads or other vegetables on the same site in a year, and remove grass clipping during lawn mowing.

It does not take long for the ground to become hungry and when it does the quality of the plants deteriorates. The best way to repay the debt to the soil is always to add farmyard manure, which contains all the plant foods together with straw for improving the soil structure. The next best thing is well-rotted plant and kitchen waste which we call garden compost (not to be confused with sowing and potting compost). Useful additional soil improvement comes from digging in a carpet of annual weeds during the course of a year. But bulky, organic matter is not enough for an intensively cultivated garden and concentrated N, P and K should be provided by modest applications of fertilizer. Additional calcium comes from the application of lime (this is only needed by soil which is neutral or acid). Peat has no food value but improves soil structure and helps to reduce alkalinity.

Lime is also applied to heavy soil like clay to improve its structure and make it less sticky. The transformation of heavy clay into friable 'loam' is the dream of all gardeners unlucky enough to be stuck with the former, and in recent years a range of 'miracle' products (known as soil conditioners) has become available as a cure. Most will do what is promised of them – but in time and at a price. Another material for the same purpose is horticultural gypsum which has been used by gardeners for a long time.

Fertilizers can be applied as ready mixed compounds of N, P and K in varying proportions. Balanced NPK in equal proportions for general use might be marked 7.7.7. An NPK compound fertilizer marked 10.5.5. would have 10% nitrogen, 5% phosphorus and 5% potash.

Fertilizers may be organic, of animal or vegetable origin, or inorganic, derived from minerals and sometimes known as 'artificials'. Many people these days prefer to use completely natural, organic fertilizers, especially for vegetables and fruits.

The alternative to applying compound fertilizer is to use a number of 'straight' fertilizers, which supply only one plant food. The popular ones are listed below:

FERTILIZERS SUPPLYING NITROGEN

Sulphate of ammonia Used as a top-dressing around growing plants, at 28 g per 0.8 m² (1 oz per sq yd).
Nitrate of soda A quick-acting top-dressing, applied at 28 g per 0.8 m² (1 oz per sq yd).
Hoof and horn Used as a base dressing before sowing or planting, at 113 g per 0.8 m² (4 oz per sq yd).
Dried blood Used as a base or top-dressing, at 28–56 g per 0.8 m² (1–2 oz per sq yd).

FERTILIZERS SUPPLYING PHOSPHORUS

Superphosphate Used as a base dressing before sowing or planting, at 28–56 g per 0.8 m² (1–2 oz per sq yd).
Basic slag Applied in autumn or winter before sowing or planting, at 113 g per 0.8 m² (4 oz per sq yd).
Bonemeal Applied in autumn or winter before sowing or planting, at 56–113 g per 0.8 m² (2–4 oz per sq yd).

FERTILIZERS SUPPLYING POTASH

Sulphate of potash Used as a base dressing just before sowing or planting, at 28–56 g per 0.8 m² (1–2 oz per sq yd).
Wood ashes Used as a base dressing before sowing or planting, at 170–226 g per 0.8 m² (6–8 oz per sq yd).

FRIEND OR FOE

A word about friends and foes in the garden – especially foes, many of which can be combated with a wide range of chemicals, these days. The foes you face are mainly insects, who wish to share the fruits of your endeavours (there are also larger creatures such as birds and mice which are not being considered here); fungal spores which alight and develop on plants when conditions are right for them; and weeds.

Some friends occur in the insect camp, notably ladybirds and parasitic wasps. While in the soil, helpful centipedes (which are more active than the harmful millipedes), certain burying beetles and invaluable earthworms are found. Any damage done by birds is compensated by their activity in searching out pests, including slugs and snails.

Before resorting to chemical control, be sure that other approaches have been tried. There is no substitute for good hygiene in the garden. This includes removing all trash and litter for composting or burning and avoiding dense, damp tangles of growth and weeds which are breeding grounds for pests and diseases. It means attending to weeding, cutting out dead growth, digging out the last remains of food crops and keeping tools and equipment clean. It is attention to detail (for which there is another phrase – 'green fingers') that makes all the difference.

But when troubles are rife, as will be the case from time to time in every garden, then go in with an insecticide or fungicide and apply the knock-out before epidemic levels develop. Even so, don't get carried away just because a suitable spray is to hand. It may be just as easy, cheaper and less harmful to the environment if, say, a few greenfly are squeezed between finger and thumb, some caterpillars are picked off by hand, or a patch of weeds pulled out of the lawn rather than spot-sprayed.

Protection and prevention are obviously wiser than last-minute action to combat a big build-up of trouble. There are pesticides (insect and disease killers) with limited persistence in the plant's sap stream so that pests or diseases arriving soon after spraying will be controlled. These sprays are known as systemic pesticides. They are best sprayed on to susceptible foliage, such as that of roses, ahead of possible infection.

There are weedkillers or herbicides to suit every need, including total growth killers like paraquat (for annual weeds) and glyphosate (for perennials like nettles, ground elder and docks) which allow the ground to be sown or planted soon after application. There are selective herbicides for use on lawns which will destroy broad-leaved weeds but which leave grasses unaffected. And there are weedkillers like propachlor which, if applied to clean ground among plants, will prevent weed seeds from germinating. There are special weedkillers for paths and gravel areas, too, which make light work of keeping these areas weed-free.

CHAPTER 3

LARGER GARDEN DESIGN

As land becomes scarcer, gardens become smaller. Anyone with a quarter of an acre or more has a large garden by today's standards. Most fortunate are those who have a *new* garden to create in an area of that size. Because undoubtedly, starting from scratch you can have a better, cleaner, more modern outlook from your home with the wide range of plants and materials now available.

If you are taking over an established plot, especially if it is fairly large, the chances are it will be cluttered with overgrown shrubs, darkened by high trees and laid-out with old, cracked and weed-infested paving, an ill-placed rockery and a dirty pond. But whether you are starting from scratch or re-planning an existing garden, the same basic principles apply.

Much depends on your situation, the type of plot, its overall shape and where the house sits in relation to the main part of the garden. It is impossible to produce a blueprint that can be applied to every garden. In the end the choice of style must always be your own.

Basically, in the design of larger gardens, we will be looking for a pleasant and interesting outlook for every window in the house, an outlook that blends with your home and is entirely compatible with it. The creation of vistas gives your garden a sense of distance, space and depth. The inclusion of special features, such as a rock garden, pond, pergola and terrace adds interest. The element of surprise, discovered by visitors as they walk round your garden gives enormous pleasure. Finally, an air of mystery, often created by dividing the garden into two or more sections, each in contrasting design, provides the final touch.

Above all, your garden must suit your own special requirements and the amount of time you will be able to spend on it. It is important, therefore, to establish, truthfully in your own mind, the type of garden you really want.

The way your garden will look eventually is not the only important factor. Study how the land lies in relation to all points on the compass. Make a note of the general aspect, of shady or specially sunny areas, check for wind tunnels and particularly exposed places, look out for damp and waterlogged patches. All of these are vital when you are weighing up where to site your flower-beds, where to put screens and windbreaks and where to build your sitting areas. With a larger garden, which may not be particularly well protected from the elements, these points are vital. So make a thorough survey, noting your findings.

Next, give some thought to the features which you might eventually like to include: pool, patio, pergola, terrace or rock garden. Again, draw up a list so that you can sketch them in on your master-plan – even if you are unlikely to be able to start work on them for a season or two. One word of warning: don't try to include every possible style and feature in one garden; the result will be that each detracts from all the others. Confine yourself to two or three really good ideas, and work on them.

PLANNING

Having made some notes on the site and listed the main features desired, the time has come to start planning. Equip yourself with a pencil and several sheets of graph paper.

Rough out, to scale, accurate dimensions of your house and garden boundaries. Then get to work on the design itself. This is usually best done in three stages.

Stage one consists of a rough plan on which to map out paving and terracing around the perimeter of the house and also the general area of the lawns. Try to nominate a focal point, perhaps a large tree of shrub mid-way down the back garden. If there isn't a focal point, you will need to establish one. Designing a garden is like painting a three-dimensional picture, it is helpful to have some object on which to take your bearings, thus arriving at a design which has balance and which is in perspective.

On stage two of the plan add the dominant features, such as trees and shrubs, walls, terraces, arches and so on that will provide and establish the outline of the garden proper. The third stage involves mapping out your flower-beds, marking the paths that will take you round the garden, and drawing in the special effects.

As the plan progresses remember to refer regularly to the notes on aspect so that all your garden's advantages and disadvantages can be fully taken into account.

THE DESIGN

Styling a garden can be compared with the way you furnish your home. It will reflect your taste. The plants and features may be the same as your neighbours, but the way you combine them will be different.

The problem of creating an original garden is more difficult on en-tirely flat sites than on what initially appear to be difficult sites – those with dips, mounds and slopes.

For these natural contours can be used – and even exaggerated – to create sunken gardens, terraces, rock gardens, and so on. So if ever you had any thoughts of grading and levelling your rough plot – bear this in mind before setting to work to flatten it.

With level sites, the special effects and vistas have to be created rather than adapted from natural resources and this requires good planning and an appreciation of the use of colourful subjects.

An ultra-modern garden with clean-cut shapes, colourful patios and terracing will look completely out of place around an older type house. Similarly, a brand new house seems to call out for bright materials and a light and airy surrounding.

Whatever your choice, it is important that when looking out from the house there is an immediate impression of space and light. Therefore the central area of the first part of your garden is best left open: trees and shrubs should be kept away from windows.

The exceptions are climbers like clematis and honeysuckle which can be trained on the walls and need not overshadow the windows.

It is also worth noting here that the roots of trees and hedges, and even some of the more hefty shrubs, spread far and wide. They will very often throw up suckers which could ruin tarmac drives or patios and should therefore be planted well away from your property. Willows send their roots in search of water and could well find their way into the drainage system, causing leakage and blockages.

On your plan you will naturally start at the house and work outwards. It is often best to aim for a paved area around as much of the house as possible, and certainly at each entrance.

A fairly substantial patio will often prove a good idea; it may be built with steps up or down to the garden itself, according to your site. It is always more interesting if steps can be used instead of going straight on to the lawn.

There are many forms of paving available. Concrete slabs come in a wide range of sizes, colours, textures and finishes – the choice is yours.

Perhaps the easiest way of planning your patio and paved areas is to map out the design on a separate sheet of paper, using coloured pencils for the right effect. The patio may require edging, either with a low wall in brick or stone or perhaps screen blocks for a higher type.

Again the choice is wide. But as with paving it is important to be thoroughly satisfied with the design before getting on with the job.

Above Maximum use should be made of vertical space by growing climbing plants. Here on the house wall is an attractive combination of clematis and climbing roses.

Left As outdoor living is in vogue, a well-furnished patio is an important aspect of garden design. This modern split-level design helps to create variation in height in this garden and containers of plants give that finished look.

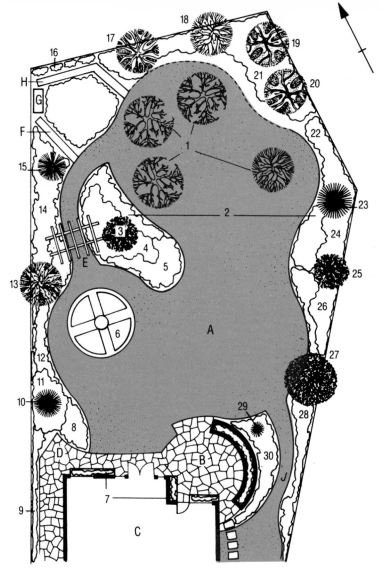

A plan for a medium-sized (quarter-acre) country garden of informal design. **A.** Lawn **B.** Patio **C.** House **D.** Crazy paving **E.** Pergola arch **F.** Slab path **G.** Compost **H.** Slab path **J.** Grass path

I. Fruit trees **2.** Low shrubs **3.** *Prunus* 'Amanogawa' **4.** Medium shrubs **5.** Low herbaceous **6.** Herb or rose garden **7.** Wall planting **8.** Low border flowers **9.** Climber **10.** *Chamaecyparis* 'Fletcheri' **II.** Shrubs **12.** 'Wall' shrubs **13.** *Prunus* **14.** Shrubs **15.** *Chamaecyparis* 'Lanei' **16.** Espalier fruit **17.** *Prunus* **18.** *Robinia* 'Frisia' **19.** *Acer* **20.** *Crataegus oxyacantha* **21.** Shrubs growing in long grass **22.** Tall shrubs **23.** *Chamaecyparis* 'Pembury Blue' **24.** Tall shrubs **25.** *Sorbus* 'Joseph Rock' **26.** Medium shrubs **27.** *Sorbus* **28.** Ground cover **29.** *Juniperus* 'Skyrocket' **30.** Low shrubs

For most people the lawn is the central feature of the garden – yet it is often the most neglected, ill-considered area. It needs the same close scrutiny as a flower-bed in selecting the variety of grass most suited to the wear and tear it will get. The commonly held view that lots of grass makes a garden easy to run is nonsense.

A lawn will need mowing once a week, sometimes twice, during the seven-month growing period; it will need treating for weeds, fertilizing, aerating, watering – and so on. If you establish a huge lawn entirely out of proportion with the size of your garden, you will have nothing but a well-tended paddock.

The shape of the lawn will have a substantial effect on the general view of your garden. A slim lawn will make the garden look longer, a shaped or curved lawn will take the eye around with it and will give the impression of size.

Don't be afraid of unusual shapes. You might try a zig-zag effect, for instance, repeated on a parallel basis each side of the lawn or, instead of running the grass area and general garden aspect from end to end, consider a diagonal approach, laying the lawn across the garden, corner to corner.

Circular lawns can also be extremely effective and better still are double circles, one in the foreground of the garden, the second in the far part linked by paths and a pergola.

Alternatively, to achieve a definite contrast between the first and second garden, use a circular shape in the foreground and a rectangular or octagonal shape in the second area.

As you move on to drawing in the second part of the garden, remember that some of it at least should be visible from the house and not entirely cut off.

Where it is possible to establish a series of gardens on different levels the use of steps can be extremely effective. These help continue the line of the house into the garden and give the illusion of greater space.

BACKGROUNDS

Having established the general plan of the garden, now is the time to think of backgrounds.

The list of trees and shrubs is endless and it really is somewhat pointless recommending specific types for unspecified situations. But the general principle is to add height and depth to the perimeter of your garden without shutting off natural landscapes and this can be achieved, even if it is necessary to install fencing or hedging, by careful and imaginative

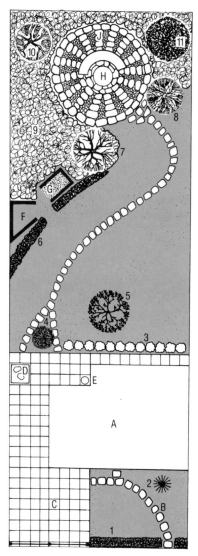

A very simple garden put down mainly to shrubs, lawn and paving. **A.** Semi-detached house with garage **B.** Sunken slabs **C.** Paved drive **D.** Pool **E.** Dustbins **F.** Fire **G.** Compost **H.** Table and bench **J.** Paved area with inset cobbles

1. Privet hedge **2.** Yucca **3.** Heather border **4.** Buddleia **5.** *Prunus* 'Amanogawa' **6.** *Mahonia aquifolium* hedge **7.** *Sorbus* 'Embley' **8.** *Paeonia lutea* 'Ludlowii' **9.** Ground cover of *Cotoneaster horizontalis*, heathers, etc. **10.** *Malus* 'Golden Hornet' **11.** *Hydrangea macrophylla*

planting. It could comprise a continuous line of one particular type of tree, with lower levels of bushy shrubs, banking down to the low-growing plants of the border.

Elsewhere in the garden – space permitting – you will want an assortment of trees and shrubs, but one has to be careful in choosing and siting trees. The charms of young weeping willows may turn into trouble in years to come as the tree reaches maturity.

You may wish to plant trees or shrubs close together as windbreaks, or as a screen for outbuildings, and in this case you will probably find that slim columnar conifers planted in groups of three or four are most suitable. One other word of caution: quick-growing trees remain quick-growing and could cause embarrassment as they mature.

The technique of repetition with tree planting is widely used. This means planting a columnar conifer, say, on each side of steps leading from one garden section to another, or on opposite sides of the lawn.

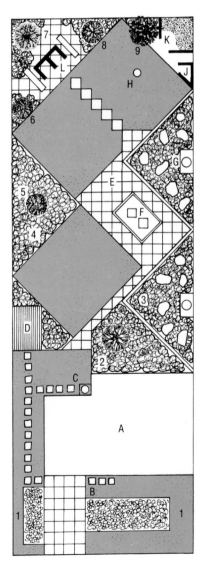

A more complex garden for the somewhat keener gardener incorporating such features as a rock garden and pool. **A.** Semi-detached house with garage **B.** Stone slabs **C.** Dustbins **D.** Garden shed **E.** Paving **F.** Pool **G.** Stone ornament on pedestal **H.** Bird bath **J.** Fire **K.** Compost **L.** Barbecue with benches

1. Bedding plants and spring bulbs **2.** Ground cover like vinca and stachys **3.** Rockery containing polygonum, *Sedum purpureum*, dianthus, etc. **4.** Ground cover of veronica, *Genista lydia*, thymus **5.** *Viburnum opulus* **6.** *Chamaecyparis lawsoniana* 'Fletcheri' **7.** *Acer japonicum* **8.** *Chamaecyparis lawsoniana* 'Fletcheri' **9.** *Deutzia* 'Mont Rose'

Before you do any planting in the general run of the garden, take a look out from the windows of your house to ensure that vistas are not being spoiled and that unwanted shadows will not be cast – in future years – over the garden or house.

PERMANENT FEATURES

The introduction of stone into any part of the garden scheme should serve a definite purpose, to raise or break levels, add a weather break, or

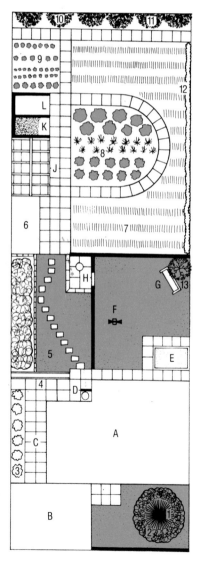

A design incorporating a vegetable area. **A.** Semi-detached house with garage **B.** Gravel drive **C.** Paving **D.** Dustbins **E.** Sand pit **F.** Swing **G.** Garden seat **H.** Bird bath on raised paving **J.** Greenhouse **K.** Compost **L.** Fire

I. *Spiraea arguta* **2.** Ground cover plants, e.g. genista, *Iberis* 'Snowflake', heathers **3.** Rose border **4.** Trellis with climbing roses **5.** Raised bed containing *Genista lydia*, androsace, ericas, etc. **6.** Herb garden **7.** Vegetable garden **8.** Gooseberries, blackcurrants and raspberries **9.** Salad garden **10.** Apple trees **11.** Pear trees **12.** Runner beans **13.** *Prunus sargentii*

make a wall leading to steps. Above all, it should fit in with the general character of the garden. Natural-stone paving, terraces with balustrades, flight of steps, dry stone walling and stone pillared pergolas are delightful features of gardens where they fit in with the environment.

But one must guard against losing beauty and aesthetic charm by the indiscreet use of stone. Try to give it an atmosphere of age. Stone can also be used effectively for raised beds. And there are numerous possibilities for low walls, alpine gardens and surrounds to pools.

PATHS

The construction of 'service' paths—i.e. those that lead from house to outbuildings, the greenhouse and so on—should be carried out at an early stage of the new garden.

The paths which take you around your garden can be left until later, but naturally it is best to get as much of the messy construction work over with before the garden takes shape.

Paths can be effectively used to help in the creation of vistas. They can lead in curves or straight lines to your inner gardens and special features. They can turn unexpectedly to behold a rock garden or other feature screened from the general view.

There should be as few main paths as possible; try to prevent them giving your garden a formal look.

BORDERS AND BEDS

The extent of your borders and beds will depend on personal choice. Certainly there will be the space to accommodate all requirements and one should remember, when selecting and designing your floral displays, that formal beds can act as a striking contrast to the informal look if you have the facility for a divided garden.

Rose gardens are often designed on a formal or geometrical plan, such as a circle or rectangle, and there are numerous other plants which lend themselves to this sort of treatment such as spring and summer bedding.

Another unusual idea in the design of beds and borders can be achieved by massing flowering plants of a single colour together so that you have whites, blues, reds, oranges and so on in separate beds.

To help reduce the amount of work involved, shrubs can be included in flower borders. They can also be used to create a sense of depth in borders by building up a bank of flowers, from tiny edging plants to tallish shrubs, interspersed with lupins, hollyhocks and delphiniums.

Try to choose summer-flowering shrubs to coincide with the flowering times of your herbaceous plants.

As with trees, the repetition of particularly outstanding plants in a border helps with the overall design.

REPLANNING AN OLD GARDEN

Creating a new garden from an old one can be more of a headache than starting from scratch.

Before you even contemplate a mass razing operation take a good look around and try to discover the garden that existed before and the reasons your predecessor had for the various planting schemes. Clear the ground of weeds, taking care not to injure too many plants in the process; walk round and cover it inch by inch and see if you can establish the original plan.

The order or priorities in which you tackle the neglected garden is entirely different from that of a new garden. Never begin by embarking on any major constructional work, such as re-shaping a rock garden, re-establishing a water garden or building a patio.

The first task is to bring the growing sections back to life. This may well take a whole season and, while you are engaged on this reclamation, the overall plan you wish to adhere to will begin to take shape. The trees and shrubs you decide to keep can be pruned back into shape so that you can get an idea of your backgrounds and colour schemes. Beware of overpruning, however, in the first year. Too drastic cutting may be more than these already neglected plants can stand.

FRONT GARDENS

With a quarter of an acre plot or more it is likely that you will have a fair amount of space to play with at the front of the house. This is not an invitation to elaborate schemes. Front gardens – unless they are on particularly awkward sites – should be simple; just enough shielding with small trees and shrubs to afford a degree of privacy from passers-by.

A fairly open outlook from the windows is called for. Properties of all ages can be set off admirably with a 'clothing' of climbers on the front wall. You will have a double viewing situation to cater for – one from the house, the other from the road.

The lawn area can be used to shape the garden and it is probable that your drive and paths will have some bearing on this factor also.

The use of trees and shrubs can also be effective in establishing the shape, and remember the repetition ingredient which is particularly useful at the front. Try, for example, columnar conifers on either side of

Above In a rectangular garden one should try to avoid straight lines in the design. Here a circular lawn gives a completely different shape to work with and creates the impression of greater width.

Right A planting scheme based on a single colour can make a dramatic feature in a garden, such as this red border which includes roses and hardy and tender perennials. Purple foliage combines beautifully with the red flowers.

the drive for a pleasing, balanced effect.

On the boundaries try to avoid hedging. For gardens of this size it tends to emphasize the enclosed look. Some sort of barrier, such as ranch-fencing, wicket fence, or heavy chains between posts, looks far more effective, supported by some imaginative plantings of trees and shrubs.

A more complex garden for the somewhat keener gardener incorporating features such as a rock garden and pool. **A.** Semi-detached house with garage **B.** Paving slabs **C.** Cavity wall with pendulous rock plants **D.** Dustbins **E.** Compost **F.** Fire

I. Heathers **2.** Rock garden containing saxifraga, anchusa, gypsophila, gentians, etc **3.** Small pool containing dwarf water lilies, etc. **4.** *Kolkwitzia amabilis* **5.** Rose bed **6.** Climbing roses **7.** Trellis with *Clematis montana* 'Rubens' **8.** Child's garden **9.** Flowering cherry (*Prunus sargentii*) **10.** Salad garden **11.** Herb garden **12.** Ground cover plants, e.g. *Cotoneaster horizontalis* and junipers **13.** Flowering almond (*Prunus dulcis*) **14.** Lilac **15.** Buddleia **16.** Two forsythias **17.** Laburnum tree, spring bulbs encircling trees

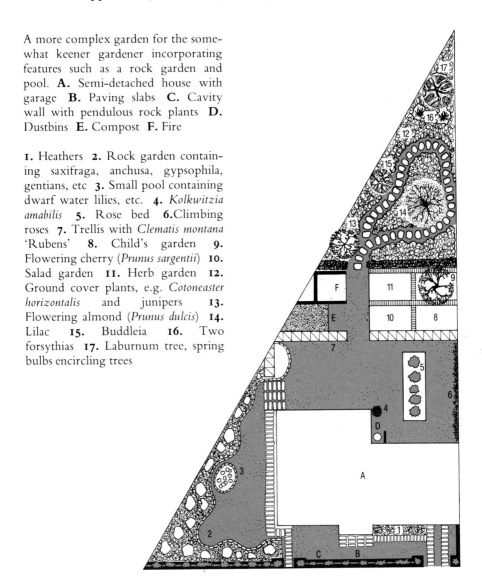

CHAPTER 4

SMALL GARDEN DESIGN

By comparison with the lavish way in which one can approach the planning and design of larger gardens, the smaller plots that are so familiar these days present special limitations – and a special challenge.

The house itself will necessarily influence the style of the garden, both back and front. Boundaries are more visible and confining and need special attention. They will also affect the design, particularly in the attempt to create vistas.

The smaller the garden the more important it is to answer two vital questions: What do you want from your garden? How much work do you want to put in? Design is also affected these days by the enforced factors in the development of large housing estates. Many developers have what can only be described as a mania for complete uniformity with open plan fronts and squared off backs – often with the same sort of fencing. It is therefore necessary to look closely at the problem of 'clothing' or hiding these boundary fixtures.

You may also be faced with hiding a neighbour's cabbage patch or washing line clearly visible through a chain-link fence. And you will want to achieve some degree of privacy from overlooking properties.

At the same time, if the garden next door is an established one you will do well to take account of those of your neighbour's plants and trees that are visible from your garden – and use them in drawing up your own planting plan.

These will need to be considered when deciding where to site taller trees and shrubs which affect the outline of your design. One word of caution. Forest trees are definitely not advisable in these confined areas. There are many subjects more suited to smaller gardens.

An evergreen shield of × *Cupressocyparis leylandii* is an ideal subject for a background. It can be topped at the desired height. Where wind is not a problem *Chamaecyparis lawsoniana* will make a good 2.4 m (8 ft) screen and is easier to control for height.

Once you have established your needs, the planning can begin. As with the creation of larger gardens it is necessary to draw up a plan of the design. Again there is no single answer or master plan that can be applied to what will be a thousand and one different situations. The basic principles, however, remain the same.

The outlook to the garden is likely to be confined to the front and back, with little or no side garden. It may be a long slim plot or a short fat one. So the task of creating a sense of space and distance, and of establishing pockets of interest which are not immediately visible at first glance, becomes more difficult.

Before planning the garden look closely at the site to weigh up the aspect – i.e. assessing to which points of the compass the garden is exposed.

Open aspects, for instance, will require screening from the biting winds, from north and east. It is also important to take into account which parts of the garden will be put into shade by buildings or trees. This is not to say that you should completely avoid causing shaded areas – these can help add depth and beauty. But you should exploit those situations that you find in your garden.

Sites which have a westerly aspect are favourable to plants which are only just in the 'hardy' category. Southern aspects should be used to the fullest extent with an abundance of plants which crave for the sun. Southerly aspects are suitable for all the most popular plants, like roses, dahlias, sweet peas, vegetables and so on. Sites facing the north are more likely to be prone to lingering frosts and generally lower temperatures. Easterly aspects will get biting winds. So bear all these points in mind as you draw up your plan.

Note, too, other problems such as poor drainage, wind tunnels and so on, so that remedial action or precautionary measures can be taken as the garden takes shape.

Looking out from the house, a focal point is necessary as you prepare to paint the garden picture. At a suitable point about three-quarters of the way down the garden, perhaps at a curve in the lawn, try to establish a fixture that draws the eye – a specimen shrub, for instance, like a magnolia, a maple, or a group of medium-size conifers. Or perhaps a pergola or arbour over a secondary sitting area. It is around some feature as this that the rest of the garden can be created.

The aim even with smaller plots is to give the impression of space. In general, one should try to round the corners of the boundaries, softening the harsh, fenced-in corners with flowering shrubs, or with a trellis, screen or pergola hiding a vegetable patch. At the other extreme do not fall into the trap of cutting out too many island beds in the lawn. They merely tend to destroy any sense of space that might be created by the lawn. One or two bold island beds are all that a small garden can take.

This informal island bed set in a lawn contains dwarf perennials which give a long period of colour and create a comparatively labour-saving area.

When planning planting schemes, try to ensure that there is plenty of contrast in flower and foliage shape and colour. This silver-leaved Scotch thistle or onopordon contrasts superbly with many other plants.

So what is the design solution to the formal rectangular plot, of say 12 m (40 ft) square, which is about the average size of new gardens today?

After establishing your focal point the major item to consider is the lawn. It creates what garden designers call the open centre – a usually level area around which the garden can flow. The greenness of the grass acts as a foil to the colourful flowers.

Avoid at all costs square or rectangular lawns. Try to create instead a

A more complex garden for the somewhat keener gardener incorporating features such as a rock garden and pool. **A.** Detached house with garage **B.** Gravel drive **C.** Crazy paving **D.** Sun dial **E.** Compost **F.** Fire **G.** Trellis covering garden seat **H.** Swing **J.** Table and seat **K.** Sand pit **L.** Dustbin

1. Rock garden containing *Campanula portenschlagiana*, arabis, *Primula auricula*, etc. **2.** Pool **3.** Irish junipers **4.** *Pyrus salicifolia* 'Pendula' **5.** Ground cover of *Spiraea alpina*, helianthemum, thymus, etc. **6.** Holly hedge **7.** Apple tree **8.** Apple tree **9.** *Clematis* 'Lasurstern' **10.** Rose beds **11.** Children's garden **12.** *Robinia pseudoacacia* 'Frisia'

lawn with pleasant curves, perhaps accentuated at a convenient point by a row of smallish slow-growing conifers, or a selection of shrubs that will tend to hide part of the garden from a first-glance.

The curved lawn will lead the eye away and save some of the features for a second look.

The front part of the lawn should be kept open, to give the impression of space. The curve is perhaps best brought in at about the middle of the lawn with a mixed border and shrubs cutting well into it – but not hiding entirely the remaining part of your garden. It may even be possible to create a second garden, part of which should be visible from the first. But, of course, this becomes more difficult in smaller plots. One solution is to screen off a part of the garden with timber trellis panels about 1.8 m (6 ft) high, perhaps with an arch built in, through which you can see part of the garden beyond. Trellis, of course, takes up minimal horizontal space, so is ideal for screening in very small gardens. Also it makes an excellent support for climbing plants.

You will need to draw in on your plan at a fairly early stage – usually after deciding the shape of your lawn – the permanent features such as a rock-garden, pool or pergola.

You can then lead your paths to and past these features and try to hide part of them from the general view from the house so that the element of surprise is introduced.

Consider also using these fixtures to hide inescapable garden eyesores, such as compost heaps, which are bound to be more clearly visible in the smaller garden. Again trellis can be used effectively to hide eyesores.

When trying to make your garden look larger than it really is, avoid using too many vistas, special features and tall bushy plants. Simplicity should be the rule with confined spaces. Don't try to have more than one or two features. If you do you will end up with a cluttered mess which will be the complete reverse of your intentions.

A curve cut into the lawn, for instance, may not be entirely feasible with a short fat plot. So try to get away from the formal look imposed by the boundaries, by making the lawn circular or oblong, perhaps with an island bed in the centre.

COLOUR CONTENT

Let us now progress to the borders and beds. Again, it is impossible to suggest anything other than in general terms. But when planning, try to aim at a mixture of subjects that will give you year-round colour – not necessarily from flowers, but from foliage and berries too.

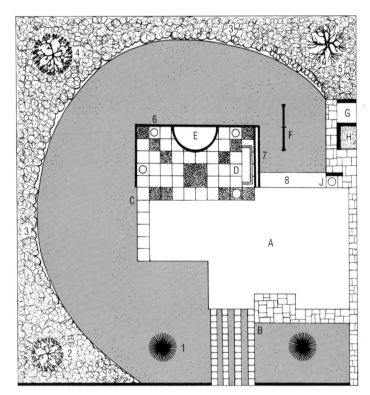

A very simple garden put down mainly to shrubs, lawn and paving. **A.** Detached house with garage **B.** Paved drive **C.** Paving and cobbles surrounded with low wall **D.** Stone bench **E.** Raised pool **F.** See-saw **G.** Fire **H.** Compost **J.** Dustbins

1. *Chamaecyparis lawsoniana* 'Columnaris' **2.** *Sorbus* 'Joseph Rock' **3.** Ground cover of helianthemum, *Polygonum affine, Saxifraga umbrosa*, etc. **4.** *Malus* 'Lemoinei' **5.** *Prunus sargentii* **6.** Agapanthus in urns **7.** Cavity wall planted with bedding and spring bulbs **8.** Herb garden.

This is important because the careful and imaginative selection of brilliantly hued plants and colourful blooms can do much to enhance the look and, in the end, style and dimensions of the garden.

The greys of lavender, rosemary and senecio, for instance, can contrast beautifully with the red berries and apple green leaves of the taller shrub *Skimmia japonica* 'Foremanii', or *Pernettya mucronata* with a choice of white, pink, lilac and crimson berries.

Again, attention to these contrasts can help in creating depth on the perimeter in what could well be a fairly narrow bed in front of a fence.

The underplanting of bulbs and bays of dwarf plants at the foot of evergreens and individual shrubs is a good way of establishing a mixed border. Although the shrubs can thrust forward to the edge of the border at regular intervals, it would be useless to plant dwarfs further back than the middle of the border.

The planting of groups of dwarf plants partly hidden by taller ones is another way of creating surprises in small gardens.

Where the planting area near fences is particularly small, use the fences themselves to help provide the backcloth to your design schemes. There are many climbing plants that can be used for this purpose. Clematis is an excellent choice – and there are sufficient varieties to provide a long-flowering season. Vigorous, fence-hugging climbing roses 1.8 m (6 ft) high or more are also excellent.

Fences like this are also suitable for fruit-growing on a small scale – using espalier or fan-trained apples, pears, plums or peaches.

SUNKEN GARDENS

If you are faced with an entirely flat garden it could well be helped by creating a change in the levels – and one of the most effective ways is a sunken garden.

The base of the sunken garden is most likely to be in crazy paving, reached by a single set of steps from the main level of the garden. The wall could be in the form of a rock garden and it should slope back to the top.

Use the top-soil from your excavations to fill in around the stones, for planting up. Plant the surrounding area in the same way that you would a rock or heather garden. The effect can be magnificent.

HEATHERS IN DESIGN

The use of heathers as a labour-saving feature is dealt with in detail in Chapter 7, but let us look briefly at the varied uses of heather in designing your garden.

Some gardens have acid soil and this will certainly affect planting schemes. Heathers will flourish in this type of soil.

In fact, a heather garden can be made on limy or acid soil where nothing else will grow. They are also effective for covering steep banks or undulating slopes and it is in these situations that they look and grow most naturally.

The shape of the heather garden should be as informal as possible and planting done in bold, irregular groups with the smaller varieties on the edge. Once established they give little trouble.

SHADED AREAS

Do not try to eliminate shade as it has an important part to play, particularly in the summer when heat may need tempering.

Many of our flowering shrubs and plants prefer shade or partial shade to full sun. They need shade at the hottest time of year to prevent scorching of foliage and flowers.

In your planning, therefore, consider well the habit, form and height of the various subjects you wish to plant, graduating them evenly from front to back, placing in the open those which like the sun and positioning in shaded areas those that thrive better in these cooler, moist situations.

The use of shade can be taken into account when you are weighing up the possibilities for adding depth to your garden. And it can also be used admirably for sitting areas.

CHILDREN IN THE GARDEN

A family with children will want, initially, a garden to play in rather than to look at, so the design can be a progressive one to allow for additions, re-styling and planting as the children grow up.

They will want at first a good paved area at the back of the house to play on when the lawn is wet.

They will want a fair-sized lawn to set up their wickets and goal posts. So the outlook and view from the house will naturally be an open one, probably throughout the garden.

But the creation of vistas can still be obtained in this garden, as can attractive beds, special feature like a rock garden, raised flower-beds and a good range of trees and shrubs. Pools of any sort where young children are to play should not be considered.

Beds of vulnerable plants will need to be kept well away from the lawn, and the trees and shrubs you choose should be fairly sturdy.

The beds can still be carved out to give your lawn an attractive shape. It is best to use heathers or low sturdy shrubs as a ground cover for close planting to the lawn. You can even walk on heathers without doing too much damage. Later, when the children appreciate the garden more, the heathers can be replaced with more colourful subjects if required.

PAVING AND PATIOS

Formal, or informal, paving is an aspect of garden making that can make or mar the finished result. Of all forms of paving, precast concrete slabs

A design incorporating a vegetable area. **A.** Semi-detached house with garage **B.** Paving **C.** Bird bath **D.** Patio **E.** Dustbins **F.** Stepping stones **G.** Garden shed **H.** Compost **J.** Fire

1. Yuccas **2.** Cherry tree **3.** Dessert apple tree **4.** Pear tree **5.** Plum tree **6.** Cooking apple tree **7.** Border of shade plants and ground cover **8.** *Fagus sylvatica* 'Purpurea Pendula' (weeping purple beech) **9.** Trellis with climbers **10.** Two *Paeonia lutea* 'Ludlowii' **11.** *Acanthus mollis* **12.** Runner beans at back of trellis **13.** Vegetable garden **14.** Cordon gooseberries **15.** Herb garden **16.** Currant bushes **17.** Salad garden

are by far the most convenient and offer the greatest scope for imaginative design. The range of slabs available is tremendous – different sizes, colours, textures and finishes – and the design possibilities are increased almost limitlessly by the possibility of combining standard precast slabs with other types of paving.

Patterned walks, patios and other paved areas can be designed to suit the particular situation or the gardener's individual taste.

Perhaps the easiest way of going about the job is to buy a large pad of square-ruled graph paper and a box of coloured pencils. Using measurements taken on the site, the area to be paved can be drawn out roughly to scale and a whole range of possible patterns sketched out and considered before ordering the paving slabs.

It is particularly important when planning one's own paving pattern to be thoroughly satisfied with the design before getting on with the job. Generally, it is better to underplay contrasts in colour or texture rather than overdo them. Use one or two closely matching colours or textures for most of the work, with contrasting areas used sparingly for accent. This will usually be more satisfying in the long term. Generally, in a garden setting, it is best to opt for natural-looking colours rather than bright pinks, greens, etc. Natural stone colours are restful, as are greys, buffs, fawns, etc.

Laying paving is not difficult (Fig. 5a). The ground should be dug out to the required level and well compacted. Then put down a 10 cm (4 in) layer of hardcore and ram it well down. Cover with a 2.5–5 cm (1–2 in) layer of builders' sand, making sure it fills all the spaces in the hardcore foundation.

Set out string lines to keep the edges of the slabs in line and then start at one end bedding the slabs. Leave between 9 mm ($\frac{3}{8}$ in) and 12 mm ($\frac{1}{2}$ in) space between the slabs and bed each slab on five small piles of mortar about 5 cm (2 in) high: one near each corner of the slab and one in the centre.

Tap each slab down to the required level with a wooden mallet until there is no tendency to rock: by using small pats of mortar rather than an over-all mortar bed the levelling will be easier and in the event that adjacent slabs settle unevenly the offending slab or slabs can be lifted off with a spade and re-levelled.

Joints can be filled with mortar which should be rubbed to a slight

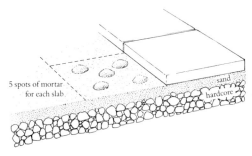

Fig. 5a Paving slabs should be laid on a foundation of hardcore topped with builders' sand. Each slab is best laid on five spots of mortar and gently tapped down.

Above One should make the most of shady areas. There are many choice plants that will grow in these conditions and here is the classic combination of candelabra primulas and hostas (plantain lilies).

Right The joints of random-stone or 'crazy' paving can be planted with mat-forming plants, such as the aromatic thymes. A superb feature for, say, a cottage or country garden.

hollow with a short length of dowel or round steel bar. As an alternative, slabs may be spaced more widely – say 5 cm (2 in) – and the gaps filled with strips of turf or with a close-growing plant: chamomile is attractive and hardy, and the fragrance as it is stepped on is a pleasant bonus.

Crazy or random-stone paving is also widely available. Broken plain paving can often be obtained from local councils. It is best laid by bedding on pats of mortar. The informal appearance is enhanced if joints between individual slabs are allowed to vary somewhat in width and if the edges of the paved area are left ragged. Too-precise joints and edges destroy the casual effect and result in something that looks rather like a carefully-assembled jigsaw puzzle. The joints, if desired, can be filled with soil and planted with carpeting plants like thymes and chamomile.

But in this instance the slabs should be laid directly on well-rammed soil. If you want to fill the joints with mortar, then lay the slabs on a hardcore and sand foundation as described earlier.

Another cheap and quite attractive path or patio can be made from old, coloured bricks (Fig. 5b). These can be readily available from a local demolition yard. They can be laid to any pattern and are quite durable. They should be laid on about 7.5 cm (3 in) of hardcore for solidity. Beware of one danger, however: they tend to become slippery during wet weather.

The sheer permanency of concrete rules it out as far as many people are concerned. But for various reasons it may have to be your choice of material for patios or paths, so let us look at its advantages as a design feature.

If nothing else, concrete is certainly durable. It will last almost indefinitely; it is resistant to weather and, provided the job is done well in the first place, it should never need repairing or replacing. Another advantage is its versatility: the range of colours and finishes available is quite extensive.

What is vital when using concrete is that you are absolutely accurate in measuring out the proportion of cement, sand and aggregate. A suitable concrete mix consists of 1 part cement, 2 parts sand and 3 parts aggregate. Or you can use 1 part cement to 5 parts all-in aggregate. Mix with 1 part water and lay it 7.5 cm (3 in) thick on well-rammed hardcore, about 10 cm (4 in) deep. For large areas, such as a patio, your best bet will probably be to buy the concrete ready-mixed.

Timber decking is becoming popular in Britain for creating sitting

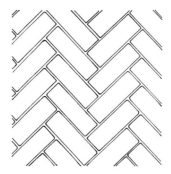

Fig. 5b An attractive path or patio can be made from bricks. They can be laid to any pattern: here, the popular herring-bone pattern is shown.

areas or patios. It is very widely used in the USA. It is low-level decking, generally raised only a few inches off the ground and is supported on stout wooden posts. It goes well with modern houses and is also a good choice for country gardens. There are various kinds of timber you can use, like western red cedar, chestnut and, if well treated with wood preservative, deal and pine. Wood preservatives come in several natural colours. You can either make your own timber decking from scratch, or you can buy ready-assembled units.

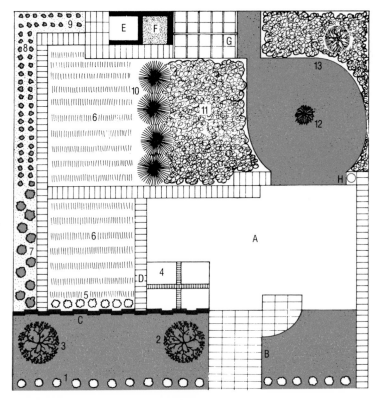

A design incorporating a vegetable area. **A.** Detached house with garage **B.** Paving **C.** Ornamental wall **D.** Paved walks **E.** Fire **F.** Compost **G.** Greenhouse **H.** Dustbins

1. *Chamaecyparis lawsoniana* 'Green Hedger' **2.** *Malus* 'John Downie' **3.** Plum tree **4.** Herb garden **5.** Blackcurrant bushes **6.** Vegetable garden **7.** Gooseberry bushes **8.** Strawberries **9.** Runner beans **10.** Chamaecyparis conifers **11.** Ground cover **12.** Pampas grass **13.** *Robinia pseudoacacia* 'Frisia'

STEPS, PERGOLAS AND WALK-WAYS

Steps in the garden can be used to continue the lines of the house and the patio into the garden itself.

A variety of materials can be used. Flat stone, slabs, concrete, logs or just plain grass. Each material will need different treatment for laying – but all will need a good foundation of at least 15 cm (6 in) of hardcore (except for grass).

A very simple garden put down mainly to shrubs, lawn and paving. **A.** Semi-detached house with garage **B.** Paved area **C.** Table and bench **D.** Dustbins **E.** Patio **F.** Sand pit **G.** Climbing frame roofed with polygonum **H.** Sun dial **J.** Fire **K.** Compost

1. Tubs containing bedding **2.** *Magnolia stellata* **3.** Fantrained pear **4.** *Choisya ternata* **5.** Round bed containing three *Yucca filamentosa* with ground cover of heathers **6.** Tub containing rhododendron **7.** Mixed shrubs **8.** Two *Cotoneaster franchettii* **9.** Vinca

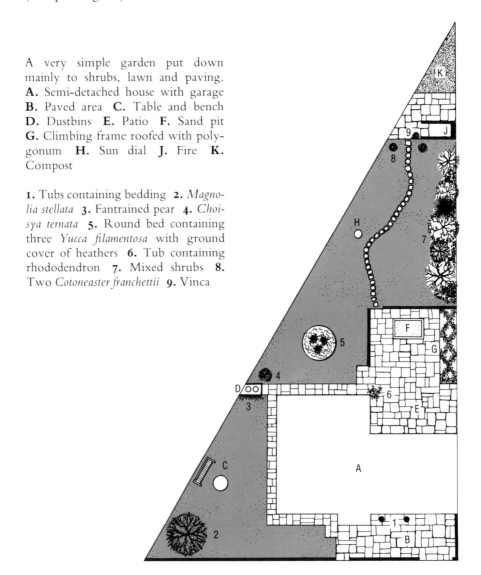

There is a place in most gardens for a pergola or walk-through arch-way. At front or back doors, or over the patio, a pergola can look beauti-ful with tub-grown clematis or honeysuckle, or perhaps a climbing rose.

In smaller gardens, the construction can be quite simple. The easiest form is one made entirely of timber, using oak or the cheaper chestnut or larch. The uprights should be set 60 cm (2 ft) deep in concrete and can take the form of a lean-to at the side of the house or a walk-way.

If you want to be more ambitious try a stone or brick piered construc-tion; the piers can be 60–90 cm (2–3 ft) in height, with room for soil around the top for planting. Or the piers can extend right up to the cross-members. The cross-members should protrude at least 30 cm (12 in) over the uprights or piers, and remember to treat all woodwork with preservatives.

WALLS, FENCES AND HEDGES

Your choice of boundary barriers should be well considered, for a bad choice will undoubtedly ruin your whole design. Fences and high walls tend to foster claustrophobia, but are often unavoidable, particularly when an instant barrier is required.

Ranch-fencing can look attractive in a modern setting as can concrete fencing. Fencing panels made of lapped larch strips are very popular and easily erected. They look good in both town and country gardens. It is important to decide what your garden really needs to set it off. The effect of stone can fail totally if there is too much of it. For screening patios and high shields close to the house, screen block walling can be used to good effect, particularly when used with factory-made walling stone as a base.

If you are a do-it-yourself gardener there are a number of points to bear in mind for a satisfactory screen-block wall. It is no more difficult than building a brick wall, but remember you will need rather more mortar at the joints and regular piers for support.

For concrete blockwork, ordinary cement and sand are too strong. Using a slightly weaker mixture of masonry cement and builders' sand – not concreting sand – in a one to five proportion will ensure that any cracks that develop through settlement or temperature changes will follow the line of the mortar and will not crack the blocks. Then you can repoint if necessary. Mortar joints should be about 9 mm ($\frac{3}{8}$ in) thick and the block should be laid in stack bond, one above the other.

Another reason in favour of screen blocks is that they can eliminate one of the major problems caused by high barriers – that of creating air-less areas in the garden that are conducive to pests and disease.

It is vital that a garden is able to breathe. Air movement is essential to all plants and assists in the moisture movement from the leaves. The moisture is taken up by the roots. If this movement does not exist, the whole atmosphere can be damp. Lawns may take hours to dry out after heavy dew; frost pockets may occur; disease can become prevalent. These are some of the dangers of absolute seclusion. So in siting your boundary

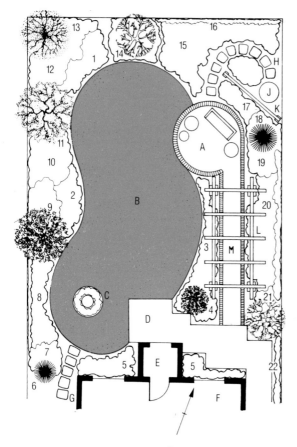

A plan for a small cottage garden – following an informal design. **A.** Shingle area with pots of plants **B.** Lawn **C.** Herbs around sundial **D.** Natural stone paving **E.** Porch **F.** House **G.** Stepping stones **H.** Stepping stones **J.** Compost **K.** Trellis and climbers **L.** Pergola and climbers **M.** Brick-edged shingle path

1. Herbaceous **2.** Herbaceous **3.** Ground cover **4.** Shrubs **5.** Low shrubs **6.** *Chamaecyparis* **7.** Shrubs **8.** Climbers **9.** *Malus x eleyi* **10.** Shrubs **11.** Fruit trees **12.** Shrubs **13.** *Sorbus aria* **14.** Fruit trees **15.** Soft fruit and vegetables **16.** Espalier **17.** Border flowers **18.** *Chamaecyparis* **19.** Shrubs **20.** Low border flowers **21.** *Rhus* **22.** Climbers

barriers try to make sure that this air movement is not unduly affected.

If you decide on a hedge rather than a fence or wall, give considerable thought to the type you want. Allow air movement at the base. Another tip with hedges: if possible run your paths alongside them. There are two reasons for this: when you are clipping the hedge it will be easier to collect the debris; and most forms of hedging require a good root run and this can be detrimental to other subjects in a near-by border. A hedge will not only affect the colour and design contrasts in your garden, but can also govern how much time you will have to spend maintaining your garden in the future. A quick-growing hedge, for instance, like privet (*Ligustrum ovalifolium*) and Leyland cypress (× *Cupressocyparis leylandii*) remains quick-growing and at the peak time of year will need cutting more often than hedges of less vigorous growth.

FRONT GARDENS

Small front gardens present their own special challenge. Because of the smallness of the area tall trees are usually out of the question since they will cut off the light from the front windows. You will be better off with a couple of slim trees like *Prunus* 'Amanogawa' (Japanese cherry) or *Juniperus virginiana* 'Skyrocket' (pencil juniper) backed up with bushes of low-growing shrubs, just to give a shade of privacy from passers-by.

One solution is to turn your whole front garden over to a special feature – like terraced paving with containerized plants – with one or two slabs left out for planting with heathers or dwarf conifers. Alternatively you could try a sunken garden or an alpine garden. Always avoid a square patch of lawn and a few dot plants in the border.

If the 'open plan' is your lot try to bend the rules by planting dwarf conifers that will take some years to grow; plant roses that can become bushier and more vigorous as the years pass (by which time those responsible for that open plan convenant may no longer be interested). Another way of breaking the monotony is to plant a border of heathers, or a herb hedge.

Finally, container-grown climbers and other plants that can be moved to strategic positions out front will all help overcome this garden system imposed upon us by the planners of our towns and cities.

CHAPTER 5

UNUSUALLY SITED GARDENS

From the point of view of the amount of work that goes into creating a garden, those with gardens on more or less level sites are at a distinct advantage over those with awkward plots. On the other hand, the design possibilities of many awkward sites are far more interesting than those of flat areas. However, the basic design principles for awkwardly sited gardens are the same as those for level gardens.

Terracing comes to mind immediately we think of gardening on slopes and in many cases this is the answer. Indeed, if your plot provides the scope for such a development, all well and good.

There is seldom any design problem with terracing a site on a slope falling away from the house. The main point to bear in mind is that part of each terrace should be visible from the top. Where possible, elements of surprise should be incorporated along the paths down. There are some sites, however, which do not lend themselves to this sort of approach. This is never more true than when a slope rises rather steeply immediately from the house.

A short wide plot that may have a boundary fence at the top of the slope, or a shield of trees, is not suitable for terracing. A different, less formal approach could be applied here, perhaps with a selection of small gardens within the whole garden, i.e. for heathers, alpines, and even a falling stream, all reached by a winding path accentuated by specimen shrubs.

Terracing on gently rising slopes is satisfactory since one can achieve a sort of rolling, undulating impression rather than strict walled-in sections. But in this instance try to hide the linking features, such as paths and steps, since these tend to emphasize the fall to the house and thus shorten the vista.

Terraces need not be symmetrical and can easily be curved or slanted. Indeed curving may be necessary if you are to follow the natural contours of the site. A long, gently-rising upward slope is better for the creation of vistas, but a downward slope offers more scope for the surprise elements.

Terraced sites, particularly those on hillsides, can present severe expo-

With a hillside garden there is great scope for attractive terracing. Here, dry-stone walling has been used to great effect. Trailing plants can be grown in the joints of this type of wall.

sure problems and it is essential to know how your site will be affected by biting winds, frosts and rain. You can then choose your plants accordingly and build in some shield features where desirable. If your slope is in the back garden the front part of the terracing can be in the form of a patio with steps out to the garden proper. Alternatively, the terracing may not be immediately connected to the house, in which case linking paths will be necessary from the flat area around the house to the rising or falling area. On larger plots, consider emphasizing these entrances to the terracing with covered walk ways or conifer-lined paths, etc.

A lawn on gently rolling sites can be extremely attractive – even on steeper banks, so long as you have the right sort of mower. But on slopes it is vital to ensure it is free of hollows or bumps – otherwise you will get scalping.

HILLSIDE GARDENS

It may seem almost impossible to establish a normal garden on a hillside. But, unless bounded by tall trees on all sides, such a garden will invariably receive sunshine for part of the day, and if it faces south or west it will receive plenty of sun.

To grow plants, however, you will need to terrace the site (Fig. 6) so that growing areas are at an angle of less than 30°. Without this it will be difficult to stop soil erosion and to enable efficient cultivation of the ground, especially if vegetables, fruit and bedding plants are grown.

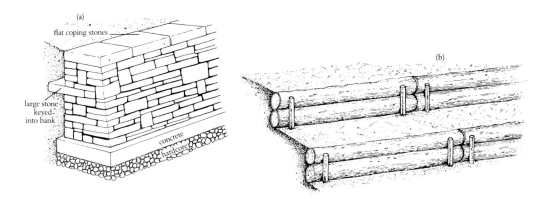

Fig. 6 Various materials can be used for terracing a hillside garden. Retaining walls can be constructed from natural stone, with soil between the joints rather than mortar (a); or logs can be used for retaining soil (b).

The use of winding paths towards the top, interconnected with broad, terraced cross-walks, is perhaps best. They will give many levels to the garden, from which attractive views can be gained up and down.

If the house is old then old brick or stone looks better for terrace walls than bright reconstructed stone or concrete blocks. One of the best types of stone for terraces is random-squared in which the blocks are of different sizes. But this is the most expensive. Poured concrete is cheaper, but it is very permanent and not very attractive.

Part of the fun of making a hillside garden is the gradual fitting of the constructional features to the landscape, so they must be flexible enough to accommodate changes as you progress. Moreover, apart from having a rough plan, it is almost impossible, without skilled advice, to visualize what the best layout will be, of both plants and materials, when you start.

Any excavation to provide level areas will provide valuable soil for beds. For paths, avoid gravel and bricks for the slopes as they are much too slippery, especially in winter. Coarse, chipped bark (available in bags from garden centres) is a good non-slip material for paths. If the paths are very steep they could be stepped, using logs as risers, held in place with stout timber stakes.

Indeed, the real answer for connecting a hillside garden is to use steps. Very beautiful layouts can be made, with curving steps, flanked by low retaining walls, with cavities for plants; and perhaps in other places the use of dry-stone walls filled with plants.

Rock gardens can be built in the intermediate spaces between waterfall levels (Fig. 7) and on the other terraces wide bays can be created here and there, to break up the general line. If you like pergolas for climbing plants, these can be erected along the terracing.

Generally speaking the garden must be constructed from the bottom upwards and not the reverse. If the gound slopes right down to a road-way or boundary at the bottom, then in order to make the first terrace – which may be the lawn and patio – you will have to bank up the boundary line as you proceed with the excavated earth and then face it with a retaining wall.

If you have to build a retaining wall you should insert drainage pipes at regular intervals along its base otherwise water which drains down the slope will be trapped behind the wall, which may lead to problems.

You can make some steepish grass banks if the soil is reasonably firm, turfed rather than sown, but they will need mowing with a hover mower.

You need at least 15 cm (6 in) of topsoil for grass and at least 30 cm (1 ft) for plants. Adequate terracing will be needed round the house to

Fig. 7 A rock garden is an ideal feature for a hillside garden, using rocks to form a series of terraces (a). Cliffs can be constructed by arranging rocks one above the other (b).

allow access to greenhouse and garden shed, for the moving of garden materials, and the provision of seating and so on.

The siting of small specimen conifers and foliage plants is particularly attractive in hillside gardens; they give that vital three-dimensional effect. Trees, however, should generally be sited towards the bottom or to one side.

The hillside and banks allow enormous scope for the establishment of mixed plantings of ground-cover plants and low shrubs, with erect shrubs and small weeping trees here and there for accent and contrast.

Heathers, gorse, brooms, cistus, hypericums, dwarf conifers, Japanese maples and no end of other plants can be used. Remember that the plants can be just as attractive from below as from above.

Rambler roses can look very effective pegged down on slopes, as can climbing roses trained to a low wooden trellis. Many other kinds of trailing and climbing plants lend themselves to being grown along the slope. Consider the new ground-cover roses with a prostrate or arching habit of

A rock garden can make a colourful boundary between a patio and the lawn. Note the use of dwarf conifers to create interest in the winter months.

growth, which smother themselves with double, semi-double or single flowers in summer. There are extremely vigorous varieties suitable for quickly covering large areas: medium growers; and small-growing kinds, useful where space is limited.

Hillside gardens should allow the maximum planting of climbers against fences and walls and on the house; and the free use of window-boxes, and tubs and urns near the house, can establish immediate interest from close range.

Generally, put such features as tall walls, hedges, arches and pergolas towards the side of the slope – so as to allow a more or less complete view from top to bottom, broken only by the various compact features at each level.

Level terraces can be paved or grassed and pools and waterfalls should also be considered as they are particularly attractive in a hillside garden.

Raised beds are also especially appropriate – linking one level to another and bordering pathways.

HILLTOP GARDENS

Planning and making a hilltop garden is one of the greatest tests of a gardener's ingenuity. The main priority is to provide shelter against gales for yourself and the plants. So the first job, after initial planning of the layout, is to establish trees and tall hedges as windbreaks.

It is not until later, when the windbreaks are becoming established, that the main plantings of herbaceous plants, roses, shrubs and bulbs can take place, although naturally the period depends a lot on how exposed the location is in relation to the worst the local weather can do. If you are impatient to plant, immediate protection can be provided by erecting a screen of windbreak netting behind the living windbreak. It will need to be about 2.4 m (8 ft) high to provide protection over a wide area, and should be supported with a system of stout stakes which support horizontal wires. This screen will also, of course, provide protection for the trees or shrubs forming the permanent windbreak, so they should then grow more quickly.

The first area to consider on a hilltop site is that which surrounds the house. This could be sheltered with trees or tall shrubs. If the slope is steep it may mean that you could only provide a flat area of ground on one or two sides.

Even if you have to construct it, this flat area is necessary because not only does it make the house stand out as a feature but it will provide sufficient level space for siting the greenhouse, garden shed and patio, all of which need to be close to the house.

The patio might be a main feature, perhaps with a low cavity wall along it, planted with the most suitable plants of the season, and adequately shielded. And it can have, at the hillside end, an arch-covered ornamental gate, leading towards the next feature, the hillside garden.

Steps, curving or straight, may lead from the patio to the lawn which, because of the slope of ground, will probably have to be partly excavated at one side and perhaps built up at another. An ornamental retaining wall could be built at the junction of the patio with the lawn, and this can be planted with rock plants in cavities left for the purpose.

The lawn can still have the usual flower-beds in or around it, with accentuating specimen trees, and could connect to a path leading to the hillside garden.

The hillside garden can have a path that winds through it, passing through rock outcrops, partly made as planted rock gardens, and rocky bluffs for carpeting or hanging plants and low conifers to contrast with the tall trees that will give the main shelter from gales in winter.

The actual summit, of course, will be the *pièce de résistance*. It will need to be partly clothed with trees and shrubs to keep off the wind, possibly to the south-west and the north and north-east, with views to the other points of the compass.

A short avenue of grass or steps, flanked by hydrangeas, conifers, or other plants could lead to the hilltop itself, where, perhaps, you might like to site a flat circle of ornamental bricks or paving, with an island bed, and low walls round the edge with seating set in them.

The hillside garden and hilltop provide endless scope for sun-loving and shade-loving plants. Heathers set in beds cut out of grassy slopes, and kept well trimmed after flowering, can make especially bright features most of the year.

If you wish to grow fruit and vegetables then these would best be sited somewhere in the shielded house-garden.

RETAINING WALLS

Retaining walls used for terracing are subjected to considerable pressure so should be constructed with at least a double, preferably a treble, thickness of bricks or walling blocks. The walls should be constructed on adequate trench foundations, consisting of a layer of well-rammed hardcore, at least 10 cm (4 in) deep, topped with the same depth of concrete. For higher walls, up to about 1.2 m (4 ft), the hardcore and concrete should each be about 15 cm (6 in) deep. Foundations must be wider than the wall.

You should leave drainage holes (or insert pipes) in the base of each wall, about 1.8 m (6 ft) apart.

Dry-stone retaining walls are particularly attractive and they should be sloped slightly backwards into the bank for stability. There is only need to slope the front of the wall – the back can be vertical, so you have a wedge-shaped wall. A slope of about 5 in 30 cm (2 in 12 in) is adequate. The walling stones are laid at random but should be interlocked for stability. Use large stones at intervals, laying them across the wall and keying them into the bank. These will give the wall greater strength. Soil can be placed between the joints for planting, as building proceeds. The soil behind the wall should be made really firm. When you have completed building, top the wall with large flat stones to act as coping (Fig. 6a).

Low walls built of peat blocks can look most attractive, but they do not have much strength. Do not expect them to hold back a great deal of soil. They should be thoroughly moistened before use and then laid like normal bricks.

STEPS IN TERRACING

There are numerous materials available, but for a difficult site the choice is fairly restricted – either completely flat-surfaced slabs or heavy timber.

In terracing, steps may have to be constructed on a very steep site and still made in a way that is entirely safe for pedestrians. The steps should not be too steep; each tread should have a few inches extra length than is normally the case, and with extra-long flights and curving ones a regular 'landing', perhaps with a seat, may be useful. The treads should not be less than about 40 cm (16 in) and the risers about 15 cm (6 in). Construct them from the bottom upwards.

Give some thought, too, to the sides of the steps, particularly on hillside sites. Side walls can take a variety of attractive forms. You could use cavity walls for planting, peat walls, stone, or formal brickwork capped for finish. If you do decide on planting the walls lining your steps, do not use trailing plants which are likely to grow down to the steps themselves.

CHAPTER 6

COTTAGE GARDENS

To many people a cottage garden is simply a chaos of colourful plants. This conveys the impression that there is no planning involved and all you need do is sow seeds all over the place. The facts are very different. The successful cottage garden is invariably the outcome of careful observation.

The basic design of the original cottage garden was usually so simple as to be no design at all – merely a straight path from the gate to the front door with two plots on each side. But there would be certain features in cottage gardens which would often dominate the scene.

An old gnarled apple tree – a 'Bramley's Seedling', perhaps – would be the largest single specimen. This would provide blossom in the spring, fruit for preserves and jellies, stewed apples for apple pies, and – a trick that sums up the cottage garden – a home for a climbing rose. Every inch of space was utilized, both on the ground and up in the air.

The art of topiary, clipping trees into peculiar shapes, came back to large gardens in the Victorian period with the revival of formalism. This, too, strayed over into cottage gardens – a clipped hedge decorated with the occasional peacock; or large clipped specimens, perhaps simple

The modern version of the cottage garden. Here an old-brick path is flanked by borders of apparently carelessly arranged plants.

mounds of yew or box, maybe with a figure on top, would be placed at an appropriate point to form a solid basis for the design. Similarly there would be two or three large shrub roses or ornamental shrubs.

The rose might be the thornless cerise-pink, fragrant 'Zéphirine Drouhin', or the old large white, 'Frau Karl Druschki'.

The shrub could be something very common – *Kerria japonica* 'Flore Pleno', known as the Jews' mallow, or it could equally well be some little known, exotic plant – perhaps a hamamelis or witch hazel or a viburnum, given to the skilled cottage gardener as a cutting.

There is no catalogue of 'cottage garden flowers'. Even so, there are certain plants that have come to be associated with the style, although it would be better to describe many of them as 'tea-cosy' flowers, the sort that are seen on elementary embroidery designs and on coloured calendars.

Yet these do give the effect of old-world cottage gardens – hollyhocks, for example, are singularly appropriate. Clarkia, godetia and nasturtium are easy annuals which give a good show, need little skill and fit into the picture.

Curiously enough, there are some plants which will grow very well indeed in small gardens but are totally unsuccessful in larger areas where they might be somewhat lost. The Madonna lily (*Lilium candidum*) is a good example.

Sunflowers, the big brash yellow 'frying-pan' annual types, are also typical – because the seed can be put to good use. It should also be remembered that the runner bean was grown originally as a decorative plant – and tripods of scarlet runners are very much in the cottage-garden tradition. So, too, are sweet peas, both the annual kind and the everlasting pea.

The old-time cottager realized the decorative value of vegetables. The beautiful glaucous foliage of nearly all the brassicas – the cabbages, cauliflowers, sprouting broccoli and so on – is attractive if regarded with an eye that has not been conditioned by false values of rarity.

These are some of the elements of the cottage garden. But it is not something that can be ordered, ready-made, from a landscape gardener. It must depend entirely on the thought, care, concentration and skill of the owner. But – given that – it is one of the most beautiful and satisfactory styles of gardening in the world.

Do not think that you need to own a cottage in the country in order to enjoy this style of gardening. Currently, many people with small town-house plots are opting for cottage gardens – and very good they look, too, in such an environment.

CHAPTER 7

LABOUR SAVING GARDENS

It is quite possible to make a trouble-free, light-work garden of pleasing design. Most of the basic, garden-design principles that have already been mentioned will still apply. You will still probably want a patio, lawns and a selection of trees and shrubs. The problem is to substitute less troublesome features for those that require year-round maintenance.

More paved areas than would normally be the case can help, and choice of materials will also affect the amount of work required through the year. Gravel, for example, requires regular maintenance. Slabs or concrete do not.

Pools can be left to their own devices for long periods of the year; rock gardens can be tedious, but again the amount of work they will entail is largely controlled by the types of plants you use. Lawns are trouble free for five months of the year, apart from raking up fallen leaves; but for the remaining seven months they will require a good deal of attention.

Perhaps the major part of the work in a pleasing design can be eliminated by careful selection of plants for borders and beds. The conventional seasonal plantings of geraniums, salvias, antirrhinums, petunias, lobelia, etc., involve much work in growing, planting out and general maintenance. Try the following arrangement as a trouble-free substitute: plant out dwarf shrubs like lavenders, heathers, potentillas, cotoneasters, dwarf conifers and helianthemums, setting them 60–90 cm (2–3 ft) apart. In between them plant a selection of winter-, summer- and autumn-flowering bulbs. In the centre of the bed plant three or four clematis, choosing varieties to flower at different times of the year; but don't give them any support. Just let them grow along the ground, spreading between the shrubs and pegging down stems where necessary. You will have a year-round colour spectacle that is hard to beat and, apart from one or two clean-up operations, is entirely work-free.

There are many other ground-cover shrubs that can be used for creating a work-free bed or border, including *Cytisus × beanii*, which forms a mat of golden-yellow flowers in late spring; *Euonymus fortunei* 'Emerald and Gold' with evergreen, bright golden variegated foliage; *Genista hispanica*, the Spanish gorse, a mass of yellow flowers in late spring/early summer; *Juniperus horizontalis* 'Bar Harbor', a prostrate juniper with grey-green foliage; *Senecio* 'Sunshine', an evergreen with silver-grey foliage and heads of yellow daisy flowers in summer; and *Vinca minor* varieties, or periwinkles, completely prostrate evergreens with blue, purple or white starry flowers in spring and early summer.

Ground-cover perennials which are suitable for filling in between larger shrubs, thus creating labour-saving borders, include ajuga or bugle, with variegated or purple foliage; the bergenias with their large evergreen leaves and pink, red or white flowers in spring; hostas or plantain lilies with superb foliage in summer; the mat-forming poly-gonums with little pink or red poker-like flowers in summer/autumn; spring-flowering pulmonaria with blue flowers; autumn-flowering *Sedum spectabile* with heads of pink flowers; the silver-leaved *Stachys lanata* 'Silver Carpet'; and *Waldsteinia ternata*, a strawberry-like plant with yellow flowers in summer.

THE HEATHER GARDEN

Heathers are superb labour-saving plants, particularly as they have such long flowering seasons, which can mean year-round colour.

They need little attention and grow into neat, colourful hummocks or form mats of growth which smother weeds. For these reasons they look well as specimens or in a mass, on flat ground or sloping sites, on cliffs and rock outcrops. Suitable, in fact, for almost any type of garden. They can be planted formally in geometrically shaped beds or in a more informal heather garden, graduated according to height, season of flowering, foliage and colour.

They can be mixed with rock-garden plants, put among shrubs where they are invaluable as low carpeting, or grown as individual specimens. They are also most suitable for island beds, highlighting perhaps a speci-men tree or shrub.

Most heathers put up with a wide range of soils, though it must be acid for most. The *Ericas, australis, erigena, herbacea, lusitanica, terminalis* and × *darleyensis* withstand alkaline soils.

Heathers must be grown in an open, sunny position. Most tolerate moist soils (indeed some relish them), but drainage must be good. All soils, but particularly clay, sand and chalk, should have plenty of peat or leafmould worked in prior to planting. These materials should also be used as a mulch, which is applied in spring.

In limy soils one can make a raised bed for heathers so that a wide variety can be grown, filling it with acid, peaty soil, and retaining it with

Ground-cover plants under and around shrubs and trees create maintenance-free yet attractive areas. Here are golden origanum, silver cerastium and 'blue' rue combined.

A very labour-saving yet colourful bed of mixed heathers, flowering and foliage varieties, and a dwarf conifer.

HEATHERS FOR YEAR-ROUND COLOUR

Species	Variety	Height cm	(in)	Flower colour	Foliage colour	Flowering season
Calluna vulgaris (Ling)	'Alportii'	60	(24)	Bright crimson	Deep green	Summer/autumn
	'Beoley Gold'	40	(15)	White	Bright gold	Summer/autumn
	'Blazeaway'	50	(20)	Mauve	Red/orange (winter)	Summer/autumn
	'County Wicklow'	25	(10)	Pink	Deep green	Summer/autumn
	'Elsie Purnell'	53	(21)	Rose-pink	Grey-green	Summer/autumn
	'Gold Haze'	50	(20)	White	Bright gold	Summer/autumn
	'Goldsworth Crimson'	80	(31)	Deep crimson	Deep green	Summer/autumn
	'H. E. Beale'	60	(24)	Silvery-pink	Grey-green	Autumn
	'Peter Sparkes'	45	(18)	Deep pink	Medium green	Autumn
	'Robert Chapman'	40	(16)	Purple	Red and gold	Summer/autumn
	'Silver Knight'	30	(12)	Pink	Silvery, woolly	Summer/autumn
	'Sir John Charrington'	40	(15)	Deep crimson	Gold-orange	Summer/autumn
	'Sister Anne'	10	(4)	Pink	Grey, woolly	Summer/autumn
	'Tib'	60	(24)	Rose-red	Deep green	Summer/autumn
	'Wickwar Flame'	30	(12)	Lavender	Orangy-red	Summer/autumn
Daboecia cantabrica (St Dabeoc's heath)	'Alba'	60	(24)	White	Deep green	Summer/autumn
	'Atropurpurea'	60	(24)	Deep purple	Greeny-bronze	Summer/autumn
	'Porter's Variety'	15	(6)	Pinkish-purple	Deep green	Summer/autumn
	'Praegerae'	30	(12)	Deep pink	Bright green	Summer/autumn
Erica arborea (Tree heath)	'Alpina'	365	(144)	White	Bright green	Spring
Erica cinerea (Bell heather)	'Atrosanguinea Smith's Variety'	20	(8)	Scarlet	Deep green	Summer/autumn
	'Cevennes'	30	(12)	Lavender-rose	Pale green	Summer/autumn
	'Golden Drop'	15	(6)	Pink	Coppery-gold	Summer
	'Hockstone White'	45	(18)	White	Bright green	Summer/autumn
	'P. S. Patrick'	25	(10)	Bright purple	Deep green	Summer/autumn
	'Velvet Night'	30	(12)	Deep purple	Medium green	Summer
	'Windlebrooke'	25	(10)	Purple	Gold	Summer/autumn

Species	Cultivar	Height		Flower colour	Foliage	Season
Erica × darleyensis	'Arthur Johnson'	90	(36)	Rose-pink	Green	Winter/spring
	'Darley Dale'	45	(18)	Pink	Deep green	Winter/spring
	'Ghost Hills'	40	(15)	Deep pink	Cream-tipped	Winter/spring
	'Jack H. Brummage'	45	(18)	Red-purple	Young shoots yellow	Winter
	'Silberschmelze'	45	(18)	White	Deep green	Winter/spring
Erica erigena (*E. mediterranea*) (Mediterranean heath)	'Brightness'	90	(36)	Purple-red	Deep green	Spring
	'W. T. Rackliff'	60	(24)	White	Bright green	Spring
Erica herbacea (*E. carnea*) (Winter-flowering heather)	'Ann Sparkes'	20	(8)	Deep purple-red	Orange-yellow	Winter/spring
	'Eileen Porter'	20	(8)	Bright red	Deep green	Winter/spring
	'January Sun'	10	(4)	Pink	Gold	Winter
	'Foxhollow'	15	(6)	Lavender	Gold	Winter/spring
	'King George'	20	(8)	Rose-pink	Deep green	Winter
	'Myretoun Ruby'	20	(8)	Ruby-red	Deep green	Winter/spring
	'Ruby Glow'	20	(8)	Ruby-red	Deep green	Winter/spring
	'Springwood Pink'	20	(8)	Pink	Deep green	Winter/spring
	'Springwood White'	20	(8)	White	Bright green	Winter/spring
	'Vivellii'	20	(8)	Bright carmine	Bronzy-green	Winter/spring
Erica tetralix (Cross-leaved heath)	'Alba Mollis'	30	(12)	White	Silvery-grey	Summer/autumn
	'Con Underwood'	25	(10)	Crimson	Greyish-green	Summer/autumn
	'Hookstone Pink'	30	(12)	Deep pink	Silvery-grey	Summer/autumn
Erica vagans (Cornish heath)	'Lyoness'	45	(18)	White	Bright green	Summer/autumn
	'Mrs D. F. Maxwell'	45	(18)	Deep rose-pink	Deep green	Summer/autumn
	'St Keverne'	50	(20)	Rose-pink	Deep green	Summer/autumn

peat blocks – which slowly decay – or with stone blocks, which are permanent.

Generally, fairly close planting of young plants is best, rather than using semi-mature plants which may not get over transplanting very well – unless they come from containers.

Compact types can be set about 15–30 cm (6 to 12 in) apart; medium compact varieties 30–45 cm (12–18 in) apart; and tallish kinds 45–60 cm (18 to 24 in) apart. Tall bush forms should be planted with about half their height between.

On alkaline soils, feed heathers in the spring with sequestrols but otherwise fertilizers or plant foods are unnecessary.

Heathers depend for their freedom of flowering (the compact kinds particularly), on light clipping after flowering just to remove dead flowers, so new shoots grow in abundance. Summer-flowering kinds are clipped in spring.

Calluna is what people commonly call heather. It is a low-growing, hummock-type plant, which hates lime, stands exposed positions in full sun and comes in varying leaf and flower colours. Main flowering period is late summer. Some have colourful foliage, like 'Robert Chapman'.

Daboecia has small bell-shaped flowers, is again hummock forming, appreciates a sheltered site, hates lime, prefers moist soil, and flowers in summer.

Erica is a diverse genus. The varieties of winter-flowering *E. herbacea* (*E. carnea*) which form mats of growth (excellent ground cover) are very popular. Limy soils are tolerated so this heather is ideal for any garden. The bell heather, *E. cinerea*, flowers in summer and autumn and is also a good ground-cover plant. With the same flowering period are *E. tetralix*, the cross-leaved heath, which enjoys moist soil, and *E. vagans*, the Cornish heath. Winter and spring flowering *E.* × *darleyensis* is deservedly popular, particularly as it grows well in the alkaline conditions common to many gardens.

Taller heathers include *E. erigena* (*E. mediterranea*), the Mediterranean heath, a bushy plant which flowers in the spring. The tallest of all is *E. arborea* 'Alpina' with bright-green foliage and sweetly-scented, white flowers in spring. The plant is not fully hardy so is recommended only for mild areas. Adequate staking is necessary until the plant is well established.

Heathers are particularly attractive in winter, with their various foliage colours, and always brighten up the coldest months, peeping through the snow when in flower. In the spring and summer they attract bees and butterflies.

TROUBLE-FREE CONIFERS

The increased emphasis on labour-saving plants these days has brought a new interest in dwarf conifers. The work involved is negligible after initial planting since most are not fussy about soil and they are rarely troubled by pests and diseases.

But most dwarf conifers are dignified little plants and hate being made to look ridiculous by thoughtless planting – under large trees, for example.

Probably the best place for them is where natural scenic beauty already exists, or where it has been artificially created in miniature. They will fit in perfectly with these surroundings, giving the impression of age and maturity that is associated with trees, yet in scale with adjacent materials.

Dwarf conifers are perhaps best used as a specific feature, rather than dotted in various parts of the garden. Plan your groups carefully so that you get the best from the wide range of colour, size, habit, and even texture. Take into account the winter colour which, with some species, is different from that of the summer.

Pay attention to backgrounds so that they are not overshadowed by taller garden subjects. With dwarfs, one really appreciates them better when they can be fully seen. None of them likes draughts – as distinct from winds – and over-dry conditions will also affect them for a year or two after planting.

The list of varieties available is endless. Some of the conical or globose forms are excellent when used in isolation on a small lawn or in tubs on the patio, while the prostrate, mat-forming qualities of the junipers make them excellent ground-cover plants, particularly for covering banks or difficult ground.

DWARF CONIFERS

Name	Shape	Height		Foliage colour
		cm	(in)	
Abies balsamea 'Hudsonia' (Silver fir)	Dense bun	90	(36)	Shiny, deep green
Chamaecyparis lawsoniana 'Gnome' (Lawson cypress)	Small cone	30	(12)	Deep green
Chamaecyparis lawsoniana 'Minima Aurea'	Cone	120	(48)	Bright yellow

Name	Shape	Height cm	(in)	Foliage colour
Chamaecyparis pisifera 'Boulevard' (Sawara cypress)	Broad cone	300	(120)	Silvery-blue
Chamaecyparis thyoides 'Ericoides' (White cypress)	Bun-shaped	90	(36)	Bronzy-green
Cryptomeria japonica 'Vilmoriniana' (Japanese cedar)	Bun-shaped	90	(36)	Reddish-purple in winter
Juniperus communis 'Compressa' (Juniper)	Tiny cone	90	(36)	Grey-green
Juniperus communis 'Depressa Aurea' (Juniper)	Prostrate	15	(6)	Golden-yellow
Juniperus horizontalis 'Bar Harbor' (Creeping juniper)	Prostrate	10	(4)	Greyish-blue
Juniperus × media 'Old Gold' (Juniper)	Flattish	180	(72)	Greenish-gold
Juniperus squamata 'Blue Star' (Juniper)	Bun-shaped	90	(36)	Steel-blue
Picea abies 'Gregoryana' (Dwarf spruce)	Bun-shaped	60	(24)	Greyish-green
Picea glauca 'Albertiana Conica' (White spruce)	Broad cone	180	(72)	Bright green
Picea pungens 'Globosa' (Dwarf Colorado spruce)	Bun-shaped	90	(36)	Brilliant silver-blue
Pinus mugo 'Gnome' (Dwarf mountain pine)	Dome-shaped	180	(72)	Deep green
Taxus baccata 'Repandens' (Yew)	Low, spreading	50	(20)	Deep green
Thuja occidentalis 'Rheingold' (White cedar)	Broad cone	300	(120)	Deep gold

PAVED GARDENS

Concrete should definitely not be used for covering any major area of the garden. It is far too permanent. The best choice for paved gardens is coloured slabs preferably in the more subdued shades.

Paving is particularly suitable for small town gardens, or for front gardens with an island cut out for planting; or it can replace a lawn in the larger garden and still blend pleasantly with an overall design.

The design of your paved garden will naturally be an open one with perhaps several areas of ground left unpaved for island beds of shrubs and conifers, according to overall dimensions. You can also have a wide range of containers and container-grown specimens.

It is still worth leaving a fair expanse of border around the paved area if this is possible so that you can plant trees, shrubs and climbers that will clothe unsightly walls and fences and give your garden some depth. If a border is not possible, revert to container-grown subjects.

Crazy paving is perhaps more suited to informal and cottage gardens. The beauty of this is that carpeting plants can be grown in the spaces between the paving stones. If you want to do this, the paving should be laid direct on soil (well consolidated) and the joints filled with gritty soil.

The design possibilities are really endless but, as with all other types of garden design, try to establish a central feature that will act as a focal point. There are numerous other tricks, such as leaving out the odd slab here and there and planting heathers or herbs; creating terraces – even artificial ones – to get away from the entirely flat look; and using tiny edging walls in a material that blends with the paving, either capped or built with a cavity for planting.

There is no reason why the gardener who chooses a paved garden cannot grow fruit trees and set up a mini-orchard. This will be possible with cordon fruits in borders; or dwarf bush trees could be grown in tubs or large pots.

Pots should always be lagged with straw or other suitable material during winter so that the roots do not get frozen. The trees you buy should be four-year-old bushes on dwarfing rootstock. Apples and pears are particularly amenable to this form of culture and you might like to try others, such as cherries, plums, peaches and nectarines.

Place apples and pears in the less favourable situations of your garden, saving the warmer area for the choicer fruits such as peaches. The number of plants you can grow in small areas is surprising. You will need little more than 1 m² (1 sq yd) of floor space to accommodate each tree.

'JUST LAWN AND TREES'

Another labour-saving arrangement that can be adapted to almost any size of garden is one in which the basic ingredients are simply grass, trees and shrubs.

A lawn is the ideal place for a small specimen tree, such as this pendulous form of the spring cherry, *Prunus subhirtella*. The shrubs in the background further help to create a delightful spring scene.

The garden could take the form of a pleasant glade which would be reached from a fairly wide patio at the rear of the house. The glade could be a wholly lawned area in which islands have been cut out for the siting of individual specimen subjects. The front part of the lawn would be left open, apart from a pair of conifers or standard roses on each side of the opening leading from the patio to the lawn.

Then there could be an informal arrangement of trees and shrubs, with the smaller, low-growing and prostrate subjects at the front allowing the outline to rise gently down the garden.

There are many subjects suitable for this sort of plan. But avoid any trees that will grow to huge proportions. At the front you could use groups of heathers, hydrangeas and hypericum, banking up with magnolia, cherry, crab apple, buddleia, *Pieris japonica*, Japanese maple, shrub roses and so on.

Around the base of each tree, cut out a bed that is the width of the branch span of the tree, because grass will not grow well here. The bed can be underplanted with suitable subjects such as seasonal bulbs.

CHAPTER 8

LAWNS

The beauty of a lawn is so self-evident that few people ever stop to ask themselves what a lawn's purpose is. In fact there are several points that combine to make a lawn one of the most important features of any garden. In the first place it is green, the most restful colour in the whole spectrum. Colourful plants show up well against this green background. A lawn is also a way of creating vistas or long views, leading the eye to beds, borders and distant specimen trees and shrubs. Specimen trees and shrubs can be planted in a lawn, and drifts of bulbs planted in the corners where they will not interfere with mowing. Informal island beds in the lawn can be planted with labour-saving herbaceous perennials, or with heathers, perhaps.

Lawn shape has a great part to play in garden design. For example, a lawn with curving or flowing edges breaks the monotonous straight lines of the typical square or rectangular garden.

The first thing to appreciate about a lawn is that it is composed of living plants that need just as much care and attention as other plants.

Many of the troubles which affect lawns can be avoided by thorough preparation of the site. It is always more difficult to correct a badly made lawn than to ensure that the soil and drainage conditions are correct in the first place.

The preparations of the lawn site are the same whether you intend to lay turf or sow seed. If you have a new garden you will probably have to clear the site of builders' rubble. Also, the builders may have carted away the topsoil, and this will need to be replaced. A lawn needs at least 15 cm (6 in) of topsoil. Topsoil can be obtained from local suppliers. It should be of an even depth all over the site, to ensure that the grass grows evenly.

Good drainage is essential, so if the site is prone to waterlogging then you should seriously consider installing a drainage system (p.17) which will take away excess water.

The site should be well dug – double digging to two depths of the spade if drainage is not all that it should be, or if the soil is really compacted.

Ideally after the preliminary digging the ground should be allowed to over-winter. This helps to settle the soil and leaves it ready to work in the drier spring weather. However, most gardeners like to get on with tasks once started and by vigorous raking they will break up the clods and level the surface while keeping an eagle eye out for weeds. Going over the ground with the heel of your boot to feel out and consolidate soft spots is known as 'heeling'. There is no real need to use a heavy roller; a light roller such as may be found on the back of modern hand mowers should be all that is needed. During the soil preparation the surface may be improved with plenty of coarse sand or grit if the soil is heavy, or peat if the land is light. Peat may also be included with the sand on heavy soils. Almost any amount of sand or grit, and peat at 3 kg per m² (7 lb per sq yd) will be suitable for heavy clay; and over 6 kg per m² (14 lb per sq yd) of peat will help light soils. A proprietary lawn fertilizer may also be added at this stage. When you have raked and double-raked and gently firmed out every bump and hollow you are ready to sow or lay turf.

TURF OR SEED

The great advantage of turf is that it gets off to a quicker start than seed. Late autumn and winter (when no frost is about) are the best times for turfing. It can be done in the spring if there is not too much drought, and even in the summer provided you can water regularly in dry weather. Turf is simple to lay, requires less-fine preparation of the soil and usually stands up better to the ravages of weather, disease and garden pests, such as birds. Despite these advantages, seed is cheaper and easy to obtain at high quality. There is a British Standard for turf, but even the most excellent turf will deteriorate in places where it was not intended to grow. Seed sowing is limited to the period late summer/early autumn, and to spring.

TURFING
Field-grown turf can be obtained from a local supplier. It should be cut to a consistent thickness and be free from weeds. If you want a really fine ornamental lawn ask for turf which contains fine bent and fescue grasses. Turf containing perennial ryegrass is better if you want a hardwearing utility lawn.

Traditional field-grown turf is generally supplied in 30 × 90 cm (1 × 3 ft) pieces, rolled for delivery.

A newer type of turf is seedling turf, which is supplied in large light-weight rolls. It is grown to your requirements by specialist producers.

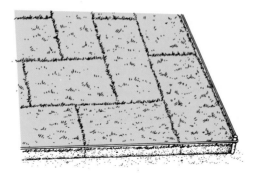

Fig. 8 Field-grown turf is normally supplied in 30 by 90 cm (1 by 3 ft) pieces, which should be laid with staggered joints.

You can order exactly the type of turf you want – even turf suitable for growing in shady parts of the garden.

Normal field-grown turves are laid like bricks in a wall, with staggered joints (Fig. 8). Seedling turf is laid in strips simply by unrolling it. Start laying turf at one end of the lawn site and work forwards, over turf that has been laid, but stand on a plank to prevent your heels sinking in. Butt turves tightly together and pat them down gently with the back of a spade. If there are any gaps after laying, brush fine soil into them.

After laying, straight edges can be cut with the aid of a garden line and half-moon edger. Curved edges can be formed by laying a hosepipe to outline the curves and cutting around this with the edger.

SEEDING
Grass-seed mixtures can be bought in various quantities from garden centres and seedsmen. As with turf, there are mixtures for fine orna-mental lawns, containing fescue and bent grasses; mixtures for hard-wearing utility lawns, based on perennial ryegrass; and mixtures for shady sites.

A finer tilth is needed for seeding and therefore you should pay considerable attention to final raking. At the same time incorporate a proprietary lawn fertilizer. Before sowing, rake the site in one direction to create mini-furrows to catch the seed. Sowing rate is 28–56 g per m² (1–2 oz per sq yd). For even sowing a distributor may be used; or use rods or lines to divide the site into square metres and sow by hand. The seed should be lightly raked in after sowing, traversing the lines of the original raking. Do not roll until the seedlings have developed. Do not expect germination for ten to twenty days. When the grass reaches 5 cm (2 in) high mow it with the blades set about 2.5 cm (1 in) high. When the grass is established this can be reduced to about 19 mm ($\frac{3}{4}$ in) for utility lawns and 12 mm ($\frac{1}{2}$ in) for top-quality lawns.

Watch out for weeds or alien grasses and remove them while small without disturbing the grass.

TOOLS FOR LAWN MAINTENANCE

HAND MOWERS

All that is needed, unless the lawn area exceeds 40 m² (50 sq yd) or you are a lawn enthusiast who wishes to cut the lawn at least twice a week in summer (which is good practice, by the way) is a simple hand mower. Hand mowers are of two types: the roller and the sidewheel. The roller type has a rear roller and another roller at the front which together ensure that the blades follow closely the surface of the lawn and so give a neat cut. The sidewheel mower has two large wheels on either side of the cutter and a small roller at the rear. It is lighter and more adapted to cutting rough grass.

POWERED CYLINDER MOWERS

These have similar curved blades to hand mowers, which form a cylinder and cut against a bottom plate, but are powered by petrol engines or electric motors (battery or mains). Powered machines are easily able to cut a wider swathe than human effort alone will allow, so the blades may be 35 or 45 cm (14 or 18 in) wide compared to the conventional 30 cm (12 in) hand mower. Electrically powered mowers are simple to operate and quiet. They are probably better for smaller lawns. You will also need a hand mower for odd corners and verges where grit and stones might adversely affect the motor-mower blades.

ROTARY MOWERS

Rotary mowers, powered by petrol, batteries or mains electricity, are marvellous for dealing with areas of rough and longer grass. The rotary mower has a horizontal blade which whirls round and chops off the heads of everything that comes within its compass. The speed at which the blade rotates provides its cutting effectiveness. Hover mowers have the special merit of making a close cut and following undulations and banks easily, and dissecting the grass into myriads of tiny fragments so that no collecting box is needed. Some, though, do have grass boxes. Some leading manufacturers of rotary mowers now fit special safety blades to their machines, so the risk of an accident occurring is negligible.

Even the most unpromising town garden can be turned into an oasis of colour and peacefulness. Note the use made of the walls, and the retention of the open centre in the form of a lawn.

EDGE TRIMMERS

Shears are the cheapest edgers and rely not so much on the sharpness of the blade as the perfection of the scissor-like mating of the two blades. The long-handled types that make a vertical cut are the most useful, although there are types for cutting horizontally. You can also buy electrically operated trimmers. Aids to edge trimming include the half-moon blade which will enable you to recut edges that have lost their definition, and both plastic and metal strip will help to consolidate an edge once it is defined.

DISTRIBUTORS AND SPREADERS

A wheeled fertilizer distributor is a cheap but useful piece of equipment as it allows you to spread feeds very evenly indeed – and quickly. To apply liquid feeds, weedkillers and pesticides, all you need is a dribble bar for attaching to the spout of a watering can. Again, this ensures even distribution of materials.

SPRINKLERS

Most lawn enthusiasts end up buying an automatic hose-attached water sprinkler. These should only be used with an outside tap for which water authority permission is needed: watering is restricted at times of drought. Extra water is usual; a few days' drought will affect delicate lawn constitutions.

RAKES AND AERATORS

A spring-tine lawn rake, or Springbok, is very useful for raking out dead moss and other debris. To speed up the job, particularly on large lawns, there is a powered scarifier or lawn rake, which looks something like a small electric mower. Aerating the soil is important when it becomes compacted and a special hollow-tine fork can be used, which takes out cores of soil. A mixture of loam, coarse sand and peat can then be brushed into the holes. There are mechanical aerators available, too.

If you inherit an old lawn it is possible to renovate it without digging it up. Simply water it with a contact weedkiller (paraquat) and the top growth will die off within a few days in sunny weather without the weedkiller affecting the soil beneath. After about a week aerate it with a hollow-tine fork. Do this thoroughly, leaving holes every few centimetres and remove the cores to the compost heap. Brush in a mixture of gypsum and well-matured compost which has been sieved. If the land is heavy increase the proportion of gypsum, making it say 2 to 1 by bulk; if the soil is light increase the proportion of compost. Grass likes a soil which is on the acid side but not too acid, which it may be if it has been used as a lawn for a long time. Test the soil for acidity and if you find it much below pH 6.5 (see soil-testing, p.16) add a little ground limestone to the mixture, up to 113 g per m² (4 oz per sq yd). Sand or peat can be added to the mixture according to whether the soil is heavy or light. Work it well into the holes and then scarify to get rid of the old grass roots. The surface should then be thinly covered with a mixture of sand and peat, with ordinary lawn fertilizer in the prescribed quantity. Lightly rake and sow the seed of your choice.

TROUBLES

DISEASES

Fusarium patch Patches of yellowing dead grass sometimes appear in summer but most often in spring and autumn under conditions of excessive moisture. The patches growing up to 30 cm (12 in) in size eventually join up and should be immediately treated with a proprietary lawn fungicide.

Corticum The grass becomes discoloured like straw with tiny red threads appearing on the grass blades. It is a late-summer to autumn occurrence and may be treated with a proprietary lawn fungicide, as directed by the manufacturer.

Fairy rings Circles of exceptionally green grass may develop due to the action of certain fungi which feed on the soil, not on the grass. They are difficult to eradicate chemically and the only remedy otherwise is to dig out the soil and returf.

PESTS

Worms It seems a pity that the better the lawn the more likely worms are to appear, because they aerate the soil with their burrowing and create humus. They are a serious problem in large numbers, however, as they produce little heaps of soil, known as worm casts, which are flattened during mowing, unless swept up, resulting in muddy patches. Worms can be eradicated with proprietary worm killers.

Leather jackets In small numbers these daddy-long-legs larvae will not be too harmful, but if the lawn is severely affected HCH dust may be used in late autumn. The larvae feed on grass roots.

CHAPTER 9

FENCES, HEDGES, PATHS AND EDGINGS

Fences, hedges, paths, drives and edgings all have essentially utilitarian functions: patios and garden walls, also included in this chapter, are less functional.

It is important to try to relate the design of a drive or pathway, as well as the materials used, to the overall design of the garden. When it comes to planning a patio or drive let your taste be the ultimate arbiter in the style and choice of materials. Before making up your mind what to do, see what other people have done: don't be afraid of being eclectic. If you use styles and materials you like, the chances are they will harmonize with surroundings.

DRIVES

Gravel, when properly laid and maintained, is probably the most attractive material for drives and has the advantage of being inexpensive to lay and maintain. It is important to stress that gravel must be laid properly. The object is to achieve a firm surface that will not become a clayey quagmire in wet weather, that will not develop potholes and that will not walk into the house when dry. The first essential is a good foundation. This should be made of a layer about 15 cm (6 in) deep of hardcore, well compacted. On normal soils this will provide all the drainage that is needed for a gravel drive, but on soggy soils 7.5 cm (3 in) drainage pipes should be laid in a herring-bone pattern at a depth of 15 cm (6 in). When the gravel is laid it should be raked and rolled until a firm, even texture has been achieved. Do not use loose gravel – the type most suitable for drives contains sand and clay so that it binds firmly together when rolled. It should be laid to a depth of about 7.5 cm (3 in). The main disadvantage of gravel is that weeds can grow in it, but this really is not a problem as they can easily be controlled by spraying with a path weedkiller.

Many people prefer drives with firmer surfaces, such as asphalt or tarmac, mainly because they believe they are longer-lasting and need less maintenance. If this is to be so they need to be laid as carefully as gravel. When tarmac or asphalt are laid over old gravel drives it is important that all loose chippings are scraped off the surface of the old drive, that the surface is re-levelled and that persistent weeds are killed before the new surface is laid. Both tarmac and asphalt should be laid at least 2.5 cm (1 in) thick. The main difference between tarmac and asphalt is that tarmac is laid cold and is porous, whereas asphalt is laid hot and is not porous. Weeds are more likely to come up through tarmac than asphalt. In either case it is important to see that the drive is properly cambered. Unless this is done puddles will form on asphalt drives and frost will quickly break up the surface of tarmac. Gaps should be left in the edgings for water to drain away into lawns or borders.

Concrete drives are long-lasting but many people find the glaring white of untreated concrete unattractive: in addition, such drives are relatively expensive to lay. They should be placed on a solid foundation of hardcore and the concrete laid 10 cm (4 in) thick. A more attractive and economic proposition is to lay the concrete in two parallel strips for the wheels of the car to go along and to use some contrasting material for the strip in the middle and at each side. Grass is unsuitable for this strip as oil drips would soon kill patches and make it unattractive, but cobbles or granite setts embedded in a weak mortar, loose granite chippings or larger chunks of random sandstone are all practicable and attractive alternatives. Another possibility is to lay a herring-bone pattern of bricks between the strips of concrete and to use parallel rows of paving slabs instead of concrete.

PATHS

The basic principles of constructing garden paths are similar to those for drives, but scaled down. The layer of hardcore need not be so deep and if concrete is used it need be laid only 5 cm (2 in) thick. It is seldom advisable to make a garden path less than 90 cm (3 ft) wide, and 1.2 m (4 ft) is usually better if you can afford the space. This width allows for the passage of wheel-barrows, lawnmowers and other garden implements, as well as for the intrusion of pathside plants: it is always a shame to have to cut back one of these plants just as it is coming into flower, merely because it is obstructing a pathway. Except in very large gardens where special visual effects may be needed there is seldom any point in constructing paths wider than 1.2 m (4 ft). In general, paths should be level with the ground on either side of them. They should also be flat rather than cambered, as this makes them more comfortable to walk along.

Where gravel is used a foundation of 7.5 to 10 cm (3 to 4 in) is adequate on most soils, but on heavy land the foundation needs to be

15 cm (6 in) deep, and on really badly drained land 7.5 cm (3 in) drainage pipes should be laid in herring-bone pattern at 45 cm (18 in) intervals. A layer of gravel 5 cm (2 in) thick is sufficient. Concrete, when used for a garden path, looks utilitarian and it is usually preferable to trying to find an alternative material. Bricks laid in herring-bone pattern look particularly attractive but the bricks must be sound or they will quickly be broken up by frost. Use special, hard, paving bricks or stock bricks. There is a tendency for brick paths in shaded situations to become slippery: the slipperiness is caused by algae: it is a hazard that can easily be cured by watering with a proprietary algicide.

Other brick-like materials can also be used to make attractive garden paths. Stable-floor bricks, which have grooves in them for drainage, are attractive and can usually be bought inexpensively from demolition contractors, as can old limestone cobbles or granite setts, both of which make exceptionally attractive paths.

When creating brick, cobble or granite-sett paths it is best to lay a foundation of hardcore and then a 2.5 cm (1 in) layer of concrete. Once this has been allowed to go off another layer of weak mortar should be laid and the bricks or setts embedded in this. Afterwards the bricks or setts can be pointed with a strong cement mixture, or soil can be used and grass allowed to grow up between the bricks. If this is the intention, extra care must be taken in getting the path level, otherwise it will be almost impossible to take a mower over it.

Paths do not necessarily need to be solid or continuous. Often 'stepping stones' in the lawn or through a rock garden are just as serviceable. Paving slabs, which can be either the old stone type or the modern concrete type, are the easiest materials for paths of this kind. If the stepping stones are required in the lawn or border all that is necessary is to take out a hole of appropriate shape and depth, firm the soil thoroughly and lay the slab in the hole. Firm the soil well around it.

Crazy paving is probably the most popular of all materials for paths. Again, either stone or broken concrete slabs can be used; both are long lasting, though stone is more expensive. To make a lasting path, crazy paving can be laid on a firm foundation of rubble and concrete, embedded in mortar and pointed with strong mortar.

EDGINGS

Though they are unfashionable, edgings are still desirable in some situations: for example, to separate a border from a gravel path or drive. There are various materials that can be used. Concrete, though not the most attractive, is one of the most widely used. It is serviceable and long-lasting, though harsh to the eye in gardens that are in other ways mellow. Concrete edging can be bought in pre-cast lengths with rounded edges. These need to be set in a base of concrete. Far more attractive in most gardens is brick, but the bricks need to be sound and hard. They can be laid horizontally as they are in walls, in which case they will need to be laid on a narrow foundation and bonded together with mortar; they can be laid diagonally; or inserted vertically. Whichever style is adopted, trouble must be taken to ensure that when they are to be laid in a straight line the line really is straight and preferably level. This is most easily done by using a line and spirit-level and driving pegs into the ground beside the line of edging to the desired height. It is usually best to use mortar when laying a brick edging. Stone slabs, faced on one edge only, also make an attractive edging, and should be laid in a similar fashion.

Wood edgings are sometimes used: these may be either wooden planks or, more informally, logs. Neither is so harsh in appearance as some of the other types of edging, but neither is so long lasting. If planks are used they should be 15 × 2.5 cm (6 × 1 in), buried to half their depth in the soil and secured to stout pegs by means of galvanized nails. The pegs should be 60 cm (2 ft) long, inserted on the inside of the edging at intervals of not more than 1.8 m (6 ft).

Proprietary log rolls are very smart; they can be obtained from garden centres. Basically these are half sections of logs, joined together with flexible metal strips, and you buy them in 1 m (1 yd) lengths. They come in various heights and are easily installed by sinking them into the ground and firming the soil on each side of them. Log rolls are treated with wood preservative and have a very long life. They look good in any setting, but are a particularly suitable choice for informal or natural gardens.

PATIOS

Patios are basically places for sitting out in the garden when the weather is fine, and as such are usually paved, either with crazy paving or formal paving slabs, but there is a wealth of other materials that can be used to provide a variety of surfaces, colours and textures. From a design point of view a patio is a link between the house and the garden and it should reflect the styles of both.

The method of laying a patio is basically the same as for a paved drive or path. There must be a firm hardcore foundation topped with a layer of sand. A patio should always be given a slope, so that water will drain away from the house, and a drop of 1 in 60 is sufficient to achieve this,

Stepping stones set in the lawn entice one to explore the secluded part of this garden.

provided the surface material is laid relatively level. To achieve this drop the patio should be marked out with wooden pegs driven into the ground to the required depth.

Because patios are essentially sun-traps they provide an ideal place for growing tender plants that might not thrive in the open garden. Whether you intend to grow tender plants or not, you will want some colour in the patio and so beds and borders should be planned before paving is laid and so should the position of any tree that is to be grown to cast shade. Beds at the foot of a wall need to be at least 45 cm (18 in) wide, as walls tend to create rain shadows, i.e. places shadowed from rain.

It is not necessary to build a patio on a rectangular plan. They are often made more attractive if a number of different coloured materials and different textures are used. Areas of sea-washed pebbles set in concrete relieve the monotony of paving and so do areas of brick.

Garden pools, often with fountains, are frequently incorporated in patios and the sound of falling water is certainly refreshing on really hot days. A bubble fountain, trickling over an old mill-stone, or at least a concrete imitation, is a popular modern feature for a patio. And one should not forget a barbeque, for alfresco meals are very much in vogue. It's nice to use the patio on warm summer evenings, when it can be illuminated with a patio-lighting set. Statuary, urns and tubs of flowers all add to the appeal of a patio.

FENCES

Fences are usually, by their very nature, unattractive structures but they need not remain so. Most types of fencing lend themselves to having plants trained against them. Solid fences are ideal for roses and other climbing plants while mesh fences make good supports for twining plants. Ivies, especially the variegated forms, are excellent for covering north-facing fences.

Galvanized wire netting is probably the least-durable fencing material, though it is not as obtrusive as more solid material. Neither is chain-link obtrusive and it certainly has a much longer life than wire netting. Plastic-mesh fencing is widely used and readily available from garden centres. The trouble is, the colour, usually green, rarely blends too well with the garden. Of the longer-lasting types, close-boarded oak fencing is the best but it is expensive. Larch, pine, fir and deal are alternatives but they all need regular treatment with preservatives and even then will not last as long as oak. Interwoven fencing can be bought in prefabricated sections of varying heights and lengths and is usually supplied with posts and fittings. The panels should be fitted between the posts, not on one side only. Fencing posts do not have to be concreted in the ground, although this is recommended if you have a light, sandy soil. Instead metal post supports can be used. These consist of a metal spike, at the top of which is a square cup. The support is hammered into the ground until the base of the cup is level with the soil. The post is then pushed into the cup. With some models, the cup can be tightened around the base of the post by means of bolts.

WALLS

A well-built brick or stone wall, particularly when it has had time to mellow, is a great asset to a garden but in view of its high cost it is usually an uneconomic proposition. Fences and hedges usually do just as well in providing privacy or hiding unsightly objects, so the expense can seldom be justified. The average gardener can easily erect a wall up to 90 cm (3 ft) on his own, but he would be unwise to attempt anything higher unless he is an experienced bricklayer (Fig. 9).

Low walls 60–90 cm (2–3 ft) high, are often used to mark the boundary across the front of a garden; they are also useful where something permanent is needed to separate a patio from the rest of the garden. Materials other than brick can be used for low walls and it is often a good idea to use local, traditional building materials where these occur; among such materials are random stone and flint (either dressed or not) and sea-washed pebbles in coastal areas.

Screen-block walling (p.55) is very popular for screening within the garden, perhaps around a patio (Fig. 10).

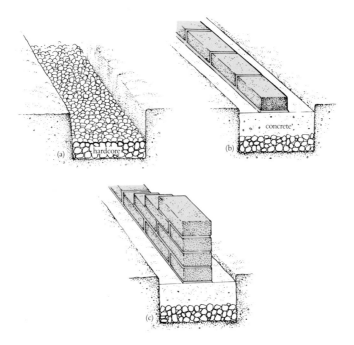

Fig. 9 When building a wall start with a trench for the foundations, partially filled with well-rammed hardcore (a). Top the hardcore with a similar depth of concrete (b). Build up the wall at each end (c), then fill in the middle.

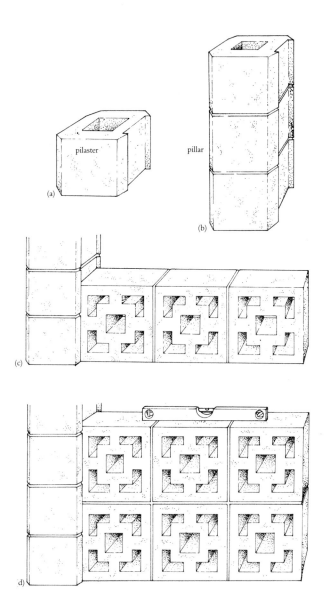

pilaster

pillar

(a)

(b)

(c)

(d)

Fig. 10 A screen-block wall is supported with piers formed from hollow cubes known as pilasters (a). The piers (b) have metal reinforcing rods through them. The concrete blocks are locked into the slots of the pilasters (c) during building. Blocks are laid in stack bond (d).

HEDGES

Most gardens benefit from having at least one good length of hedge, whether to provide shelter from cruel winds, privacy, a background to a border or simply because a well-kept hedge is a joy in itself. The problem with a formal hedge is that it needs regular trimming, although this can be speeded up considerably if an electric hedge-trimmer is used.

A formal hedge should be wedge-shaped – narrower at the top than at the bottom. Ideally, the top should be rounded to shed snow.

Needing no attention (apart, perhaps, from reducing in length any over-long shoots) is the informal hedge, which generally consists of a flowering shrub such as *Berberis darwinii, Berberis* × *stenophylla* or, in mild and coastal areas, escallonia. However, an informal hedge takes up a lot of space so is unsuitable for a small garden.

Hedging plants are planted in a row, spacing them, on average, 45–60 cm (18–24 in) apart, depending on vigour.

Of the plants recommended for formal hedging, privet is probably the most ubiquitous. It is cheap, easily raised from cuttings and relatively fast-growing. It withstands clipping well, does not suffer from winds and will grow in practically any soil and situation. Its disadvantages are that it is apt to lose its leaves in winter, needs clipping at least three times a year, preferably four times, and that it has greedy roots which rob plants growing close to it. Common privet is a dull green, but golden privet is cheerfully bright and particularly useful for planting in shaded situations. The two can be intermixed, either planted alternately or planted two of golden privet to one of green.

Beech makes a more permanent hedge and is usually recommended where a taller hedge is required: 2.4–3 m (8–10 ft). It thrives in all soils, including chalk, and stands clipping well, normally needing clipping only once a year. It is valued for the fresh green of the new leaves as they appear in spring and for the russet colouring of its leaves in autumn. These are retained through the winter. Apart from the green-leaved beech there is a purple-leaved form, and the well-known copper-beech with leaves of a lighter colour than those of the purple beech. Beech hedges may be composed either of all green-leaved plants or of these intermixed with the coloured-leaf forms. Hedges made entirely of copper or purple beech tend to look rather heavy. Another plant suited to almost all soils is hornbeam, which is often confused with beech: indeed, it is so like beech that many so-called beech hedges are in fact composed of hornbeam.

Evergreen hedges have the advantage of maintaining privacy throughout the winter. They may be composed of either broadleaved shrubs such as holly, or of coniferous shrubs such as yew or cupressus. Of the broad-leaved evergreens there can be little doubt that holly makes the most attractive hedge particularly if it is allowed to grow tall – say to 3.6 m (12 ft). Such a hedge is practically impenetrable by winds or animals. Moreover, being a European native, it is absolutely hardy in even the coldest areas. The usual objection against holly is that the fallen leaves, with their persistent sharp spines, are liable to puncture tender fingers when weeding unsuspectingly in the garden. This need not be a draw-back; there are forms which are virtually spineless. The common holly has dark, shining green leaves, but there are forms with foliage variegated either gold or white, and these make more colourful hedges. It is not advisable to mix green and variegated forms since they have different rates of growth.

Laurel, though often used, is really only suitable for gardens of the largest size. To look good it needs room to grow and should be at least 2.4 m (8 ft) tall. Its main problem, apart from the space it requires, is that it needs to be trimmed by hand, each shoot being cut with secateurs; if cut with shears or electric trimmers the leaves that have been cut in half will turn brown and spoil the appearance of the hedge. And it has greedy roots: nothing worth while will grow within 3 m (10 ft) of a laurel hedge.

Yew makes a particularly attractive, long-lived, formal hedge. It is favoured not because of the slowness of its growth, but because it makes a particularly neat hedge and stands trimming well. It is extremely hardy, will grow on all soils including chalk and makes an excellent hedge any-thing from 1–6 m (3–20 ft) high. There are few other backgrounds that show off the colours of a herbaceous border or rose beds better than a well-clipped yew hedge. There are forms with golden leaves and these look good either mixed with green yew or on their own. Yew is poisonous to animals and this should be borne in mind when planting a yew hedge or disposing of the clippings.

INDEX